CRICUT EXPLORE 3 HANDBOOK

A Dummy's-Manual To Mastering Cricut Explore Air 3, and Cricut Design Space with In-Depth Project and Tips

Shelli Lynne

Contents

Combine:

Attach:

Flatten:

Contour:

Color Sync Panel:

How to Change Canvas Color:

INTRODUCTION

In this day and age of limitless options and creation, the Cricut Explore 3 is a truly amazing tool that has changed the game for artists and crafters.

You can use this machine to make many creative projects and beautiful designs, and this Handbook will take you on a journey to learn how to use the Explore 3 machine.

As you turn these pages, you're not just reading a book – you're embarking on a self-discovery journey where your ideas will come alive, and your creativity has no limits.

CHAPTER ONE

The Cricut Machine

I've always had trouble cutting things quickly and accurately, even though I love making projects. I would cut out complicated patterns with scissors and an X-acto knife for hours at a time, and my hands would often hurt afterward.

I came across the Cricut Explore 3 while browsing the web one day. It was a cutting machine that claimed to make crafting easier and faster.

This cutting material seems interesting, so I decided to give it a try. Truly, it has been worth my money because it has made crafting easy for me, and I simply love it.

What Can I Make With Explore 3?

With the Explore Air 3, you can make an incredibly large amount of different projects. You can make your artistic ideas come to life with precision and ease with this cutting machine. Some things you can make are:

- **Custom Apparel:** You can make t-shirts, hoodies, hats, and other items more unique. You can also make iron-on stickers for shoes, bags, and other items.

- **Home Decor:** You can make vinyl writing, cutouts, and wall stickers for your pillows, signs, and other home decor items.

- **Paper Crafts:** You can make welcome cards, notes, paper flowers, and decorations for scrapbooks that are very complicated.

- **Party Decorations:** You can also design banners, centerpieces, cake toppers for your party and giveaway treats.

- **Kids' Crafts and Educational Materials:** You can make puzzles, flashcards, educational games, and interactive storyboards.

These are just a few ideas of what you can make with the Cricut Explore Air 3. The possibilities are endless!

CHAPTER TWO
New Features of Explore 3

There are new and better features on the Cricut Explore 3 that make making more fun and give users more ways to be artistic. You will learn about the new Cricut Design Space features in this chapter.

What's New:

The Cricut Explore 3 is a powerful tool that caters to crafters of all levels. It is designed to streamline the creative process and provide even more precision. Here is a summary of what's new in the Cricut Explore 3 machine:

(1) Design: The Cricut Explore 3's body design makes it a beautiful craft machine that can be used in any environment. The sewing machine is beautifully designed to take up very little space in your room.

It's only 15 x 17 x 56 cm, so it is easy to store and move around. It weighs only 10 pounds, which is about half as light as the Cricut Maker 3. There is a small LCD screen and several buttons on the front of the machine that let you change settings and use its features.

(2) Cut Numerous Materials: You can cut a lot of different materials with the Cricut Explore 3. It can cut through paper, cardstock, vinyl, iron-on, fabric, and even thicker materials like balsa wood and leather. Because of this, the designs you can make with it are almost limitless.

(3) Compatible with Smart Materials: Smart Materials are made to work perfectly with the Explore Air 3, so you don't need a cutting mat to quickly cut and clear them.

Smart Materials come in many shapes and sizes, and they're great for making complicated designs without having to cut or stack them many times.

The Explore Air 3 can cut Smart Materials that are up to 12 feet long and 11.7 inches thick. It's great for bigger jobs like posters and signs because of this. The machine will figure out what it's cutting and change its settings automatically to make sure every cut is perfect.

(4) Speed and Precision: Only a few users have noticed a change in speed between the Cricut Explore Air 3 and its predecessor, the Cricut Explore Air 2. One difference is that the Explore Air 3 can cut up to 8 inches per second, while the Cricut Explore Air 2 can only cut up to 7.9 inches per second.

The speed difference isn't very big, but you might notice it when you're making bigger or more complicated shapes. The Explore Air 3 also has a better adaptable tool system that lets the machine instantly change the cutting speed and pressure for different fabrics.

(5) Bluetooth and Wireless Technology:

The Explore Air 3 uses Bluetooth with its cordless technology that helps users in several ways. You don't need cords or wires to connect your Cricut Explore Air 3 to your computer, tablet, or phone when you use Bluetooth.

This lets you move your computer around more easily and gets rid of the need for a separate desk. You can also work with your Cricut Explore Air 3 from farther away with Bluetooth than with a USB cord. This gives you more options for how to use your machine.

These are some of the new features that are included in the new Cricut Explore 3. In subsequent chapters, you'll learn how to get started.

CHAPTER THREE

Getting Started

There's something satisfying about unwrapping the packaging and revealing the sleek, stylish design of the Cricut Explore Air 3.

Unboxing Cricut Explore Air 3:

It can be very exciting to wait for your new Explore Air 3 to come and then feel great when it does. These are the things that were in the box:

Welcome Packet: The welcome packet contains the following items;

1. The Get Started Manual,

2. Sample Vinyl

3. Warranty

4. Safety Papers.

Sample Materials: The sample material include the following items;

1. Removable Vinyl

2. Transfer Tape

3. Iron On

4. Sticker Cardstock

5. Cardstock in White.

Cricut Explore 3: This is the machine for making designs and cuts.

Cable: You can find a USB-C Cable and Charging Cord inside the box.

NOTE: It is important to know that the Cricut Explore 3 doesn't come with a cutting mat because it has smart materials built in.

Unboxing Tips & Tricks:

Here are some unboxing tips to help you properly handle and care for your new item:

Inspect the Box: Check the box for damage from the shipping process before you open it. If you see any damage, take pictures of both the box and the place that is broken.

Unpack Carefully: Take your time and be careful as you unpack the item to keep it from getting broken. Use something sharp like a knife to open the box.

Keep Packaging: Save all the boxes and tape in case you need to return or store the thing later.

Read Instructions: Carefully read any directions or user guides that come with the item before you use it.

Remove Protective Covers: Some things may come with covers or sheets to keep them safe. Being careful not to hurt or scratch anything, take these off slowly.

Check for Accessories: Some things might come with covers or sheets to keep them safe. Take these off carefully so that they don't get damaged or scratched.

Organize Cords and Cables: Be careful not to damage or tangle cords and wires when you handle them. Twist ties or wire wraps can help you keep them in order.

Clean and Care: Follow the manufacturer's advice to clean the item and any parts that come with it before you use them.

Choose a workspace: When setting up your Cricut Explore 3, make sure the area is clean, dry, level, and free of clutter. It should also have enough space for the machine, your laptop or computer, and any other tools or extras you might need.

Use a protective mat: Use a protected mat or surface under the Cricut Explore 3 to keep your work area safe. This will keep the table or desk from getting scratched or damaged.

Ensure proper ventilation: When you use the Cricut Explore 3, it may give off some heat and smell, so make sure your area has enough air flow to keep you comfortable and protect the machine.

Position the machine correctly: The Cricut Explore 3 should be put somewhere that is easy to get to and use. It should be put somewhere that makes it easy to get to your computer, laptop, and any other papers or tools you might need.

Components of Explore Air 3:

Here are the key components of explore air 3 and their functions:

Button: There are four buttons on top of the Cricut machine that let you control it or move it around:

- Power Button: This button turns the machine on and off.

- Go Button: This button is used to start the cutting process.

- Pause Button: This button allows you to stop the cutting process.

- Direction Button: Before cutting, the direction buttons assist make slight blade adjustments. Up arrow button raises carriage and blade housing to machine top. The down arrow button lowers the carriage and blade housing.

Carriage: The carriage holds the cutting blade and moves across the mat to cut the material.

Blade Housing: The blade housing is located in the carriage and holds the cutting blade. The Cricut Explore Air 3 comes with a fine-point blade for cutting most materials.

Tool Holder: The tool holder is located on the side of the machine and holds various tools such as the scoring stylus or pen.

Cutting Mat: The cutting mat holds the material in place while the machine cuts. The Explore Air 3 comes with a standard grip mat that can cut most materials.

USB Port: The USB port is located on the back of the machine and can be used to connect the machine to a computer.

Display Screen: The display screen is located on the top of the machine and shows information about the selected material and cutting settings.

Frequently Asked Questions (FAQ):

Here are some frequently asked questions about the Cricut Explore Air 3:

What materials can the Cricut Explore Air 3 cut?

The Cricut Explore Air 3 can cut over 100 materials, including: Cardstock, Vinyl, Iron-on, HTV, Paper, Fabric, Wood, Leather, Felt, Foam, etc.

What is Design Space?

Design Space is the software that you use to create your projects. It is a free software that you can download on your computer or mobile device.

How do I get started with the Cricut Explore Air 3?

The first thing you need to do is create an account on Cricut.com. Once you have an account, you can download Design Space.

To get started with a project, you can either upload your own design or use a design from the Cricut library. Once you have your design, you need to select the materials you want to cut and the settings you want to use.

Thereafter, you can send your project to the Explore Air 3 and the machine will cut your project according to your instructions.

Difference between Explore Air 3 and Maker 3?

The Maker 3 is more sophisticated than the Explore Air 3 because it can cut leather, wood, and other heavier materials with it rotating and knife blades.

Difference between Explore 3 and previous models?

New features in the Cricut Explore 3 include faster cutting mode, an adaptive tool system for automatic pressure adjustments, Bluetooth connectivity, a wider range of materials that can be used, an EasyLoad mat and tool tray, and better precision cutting and scoring.

Can I use my smartphone or tablet with the Cricut Explore 3?

Yes, the Cricut Explore 3 does have Bluetooth connection, so you can use your phone, tablet, or computer to connect to it. With this tool, you can create and cut right from your phone.

Is the Smart Set Dial still present on the Cricut Explore 3?

No, there is no longer a Smart Set Dial. Instead, there is an automatic method for choosing materials. The machine figures out what kind of cloth you're using and offers the right settings, so you don't have to change them by hand.

How does the EasyLoad mat and tool tray work?

EasyLoad mat keeps materials safely in place while cutting, so you don't have to use tape or glue. The tool tray makes it easy to store your cutting tools and keeps everything in order and within reach.

Can I still use my own designs with the Cricut Explore 3?

Yes, you can use your own drawings with the Cricut Explore 3 after adding them to Cricut Design Space. You can change the size, shape, and order of your patterns in the program before you cut them out.

Can I access ready-made designs and projects for the Cricut Explore 3?

In Design Space, Cricut does have a huge library of ready-made patterns, fonts, and projects. Crafters who want to make a variety of projects can get ideas and useful information from this source.

Can I use the Cricut Explore 3 for commercial purposes?

Yes, you can use the Cricut Explore 3 for business reasons, like selling things you make with it. However, make sure you read and follow Cricut's rules and standards for business use.

Does the Cricut Explore 3 come with a warranty?

Yes, the Cricut Explore 3 usually comes with a protection from the company that covers some problems and flaws. It is suggested that you look over the specific guarantee terms offered by Cricut or the store where you bought the machine.

CHAPTER FOUR

Initial Setup

This section will show you how to connect the Cricut Explore 3 to your computer or mobile device, load the software, and do a few other things to get it ready to use.

How to Setup Cricut Explore 3:

Setting up a Cricut can be hard at first, but this guide and the notes that come with your machine will make it easy. You'll be able to set up your device in no time.

These are the steps you need to take to setting up your Explore 3 Machine;

- Plug the power cable at the back of the Cricut machine and connect it to a power outlet.

- Ensure to press the *"Power Button"* to turn ON the Cricut machine.

- The next step is to proceed to the official website of Cricut (https://design.cricut.com/#/set up) to start the initial setup.

- You can select a product type to set up on the official website. Ensure to select *"Cricut Machine."*

- Next, you must select the product you want to set up. Ensure to select *"Cricut Explore Family."*

- In the next section, you must agree to Cricut's Terms of Use and Privacy Policy. Ensure to tick the checkbox and select the *"Download"* button to install the Cricut app.

- After downloading and Installing the Cricut app, you must open it. A new window will open, asking you the type of setup you want. Ensure to Select "***New product Setup***."

- The next step is to select the Cricut machine you are about to set up. Select "***Smart cutting machine***" and then click on "***Explore 3***." (Ensure your connections are intact as you follow the prompt with the design space).

- An on-screen window will guide you on how to set up your workspace and connect your Cricut to your Computer.

- Next, you must enter your Cricut ID or create a Cricut ID if this is the first time you have created one to register your machine.

- In the next section, you will be prompted to *"Agree to the Terms of Use of Cricut."* Click on the "Continue button" to Update and Register your Cricut to your Design space account.

- After rebooting, your Design Space app will display a successful connection. Ensure to click on the *"Next"* button.

- Next, you will be prompted to *"Start your Free Trial."* You can skip this process by selecting *"No Thanks."*

Tips and Tricks:

Here are some tips and tricks for setting up and using the Cricut Explore 3:

- **Choose the right location:** *To set up your Cricut Explore 3 machine, find a large, well-lit room before you start.*

- **Update the firmware:** *You can check for software updates on your computer or phone by connecting your Cricut Explore 3 to it.*

- **Register your machine:** *You can register your Explore 3 online to get access to software changes, design tools, and resources for fixing problems.*

- **Use the correct blade:** *The Cricut Explore 3 has different blades that are made to cut different kinds of materials. It is important to use the right blade for the job so you get the best results.*

- ***Use the right mat:*** *The Cricut Explore 3 comes with several kinds of mats, each made for a particular type of material.*

- ***Adjust the settings:*** *You can change a number of settings on the Cricut Explore 3 to get the best cuts. Change the settings around until you find the best one for your job.*

- ***Practice Regularly:*** *It's easy to use the Cricut Explore 3 to cut a lot of different materials. You will get better at using the machine and finish your work faster if you do it more often.*

CHAPTER FIVE

Cricut Workspace Setup

Having a well-organized work area is very important when using the Cricut Explore 3. No matter how much experience you have as a creator.

Getting enough light and spending money on a good cutting mat are just two of the tips and tricks that can help you make the most of your desk when using the Cricut Explore 3.

In this chapter, we will talk about some of the most important parts of setting up your workspace.

Workspace Setup:

Here are some tips to help you make the most of your cricut workspace setup:

Clear the Clutter: A big part of getting your area ready to use the Cricut Explore 3 is getting rid of the junk. Clutter can be many things, like stacks of paper or craft tools that aren't being used. It can build up quickly and make your desk feel crowded and messy.

Getting rid of the mess means getting rid of anything that isn't needed for your making projects, or that doesn't help keep your desk clean and organized. Cleaning up has many benefits, such as making it easier to concentrate on your work and making you more productive overall.

Storage Area: You need a specific place to store your Cricut tools to keep everything organized and easy to find. It's easier to find what you need and less likely to lose things when everything has its own place.

When picking a place to store your Cricut-related items, it's important to pick one that is easy to get to and has enough room for everything. This could be a closet, shelf, or box that is just for your machine, blades, mats, and other parts.

Quality Cutting Mat: Getting a good cutting mat is important if you want to make accurate cuts and keep your Cricut Explore 3 machine in good shape.

The strong grip of a good cutting mat will keep your materials in place, making it less likely that they will slip or move while you cut. Different mats have different amounts of grip and binding power, and they come in different sizes to fit a range of project sizes.

Use a Comfortable Chair: Long amounts of time spent sitting in a chair that doesn't fit right can lead to back pain, neck strain, and other discomforts. A soft chair, on the other hand, gives you the support you need to keep good posture and avoid these issues.

When choosing a chair for your office, look for one that is ergonomically made and has features that can be adjusted to fit your body.

Look for chairs with a soft seat cushion, arms that can be adjusted, and good back support. A chair with a seat that lets air flow through it can also help you stay comfortable and avoid sweating for long amounts of time.

Adequate Lighting: Good lighting not only lets you see what you're doing, but it also keeps your eyes from getting tired and makes sure you make clean cuts. If the lighting is right, you might notice small but important details, which could lead to mistakes on the job.

To make a well-lit office, you might want to use both natural and artificial light. Natural light is great for evenly and brightly lighting a room, while artificial light can help to add to and improve the lighting in your workspace.

Nearby Trash Can: A lot of trash is made by this cutting machine, like vinyl bits, paper pieces, and glue residue. If there isn't a trash can nearby, these things can quickly pile up, making the area look messy and possibly damage the machine.

If you keep a trash can close by, you can quickly and easily eliminate any trash while you work, without stopping your creativity flow. So, your desk stays clean, and you're less likely to make mistakes or have accidents because of the mess.

Keep your Computer/Mobile Device Nearby: If you have your computer or phone close by, the Cricut create Space software makes it easy to create and change your projects. The software is available on both computers and phones. You can make your own patterns or use models that have already been made in this software to cut plastic, paper, and fabric, among other things.

CHAPTER SIX

Crafting Your First Cricut Project

Welcome to the world of Cricut Explore! As a beginner, you may feel overwhelmed by the number of possibilities that this amazing machine offers. But don't worry; creating your first Cricut Explore project is easier than you think.

In this chapter, we will guide you through the process of creating your first project step-by-step. You will learn about the essential tools and materials you need, how to set up your Cricut Explore machine, and how to use Cricut Design Space software to bring your ideas to life.

By the end of this chapter, you will better understand the basics of Cricut Explore and be ready to embark on your creative journey. So, let's get started and unleash your creativity with Cricut Explore!

Things to Know to Get Started:

With the basics in mind, you are ready to begin creating amazing projects with your Cricut Explore 3. Here are some things you need to know to get started:

(1) Turn ON the Cricut Machine:

Turning on your Cricut Explore 3 is the first step in setting up the machine and beginning your crafting projects. To turn on your Cricut Explore 3, you will need to have the following components assembled and connected:

- **Power cord:** Connect one end of the power cord to the back of the machine and the other end to a power outlet.

- **USB cable:** Connect one end of the cable to the back of the machine and the other to your computer or mobile device. Alternatively, you can use a Bluetooth Wireless connection.

- Once you have assembled and connected these components, locate the power button on the right side of the machine. Press and hold the power button until the machine beeps.

- The machine will then begin calibrating and preparing for cutting.

(2) Check the Accessory Clamp:

The accessory clamp which is also known as adaptive tool system is the driving force of the Cricut machine. There are basically two major tools in this section;

Clamp A: The function of Clamp A in Cricut Explore 3 is to hold the various cutting tools used by the machine to cut and score materials. Clamp A is located on the left side of the machine. Usually, the accessory adapter is pre-installed in accessory Clamp A

It is designed to securely hold the cutting tool in place while it moves back and forth across the cutting mat. The machine's software will automatically adjust the cutting settings based on the selected tool to ensure precise cuts.

Clamp B: This is one of the two tool clamps that hold the specialized cutting and scoring tools used by the machine. The primary function of Clamp B is to hold the scoring wheel or double scoring wheel, which is used to create precise creases in paper and cardstock for folding and creating 3D projects.

When using the scoring wheel or double scoring wheel, the machine applies pressure to the material to create a deep crease without cutting through it. This allows for clean, sharp folds that add a professional touch to crafting projects.

The scoring wheel or double scoring wheel is essential for projects that involve making boxes, cards, and other folded paper designs. In addition to the scoring wheel or double scoring wheel, Clamp B can also hold other specialized tools, such as the perforation blade or wavy blade.

The perforation blade creates tearable edges that are perfect for making tickets, raffle coupons, and other perforated items, while the wavy blade creates a decorative edge that adds a unique touch to designs.

Tips: *To remove or replace the accessory adapter for your Cricut Explore 3, follow these steps:*

- *Make sure your machine is turned off and unplugged from the power source.*

- *Locate the accessory adapter (Clamp A or Clamp B) that you want to replace.*

- *Gently press the release button on the accessory adapter to release it from the clamp. The release button is located on the top of the adapter and may be marked with a small arrow or icon.*

- *While holding the release button, gently pull the accessory adapter out of the clamp.*

- *To replace the accessory adapter, simply align it with the clamp and gently push it in until it clicks into place. Make sure the release button clicks back into place and the adapter is secure in the clamp.*

- *It is important to note that the accessory adapter is designed to hold pens and markers, not cutting blades. Cutting blades should always be placed in Clamp A or Clamp B, depending on the type of blade being used.*

(3) Cricut Design Space on your Computer:

The next step is to launch the Cricut Design Space app on your computer or tablet. A few easy actions will be required of you to register the computer and set up your account if you have not done so before.

With Design Space, you can create projects for various purposes, including vinyl decals, iron-on transfers, paper crafts, and more. Some of the features that you can explore with Design Space include:

Easy-to-use design tools: Design Space offers a wide variety of tools for creating and editing your designs, including text, shapes, and images. You can also import your own images or use designs from the Cricut library.

Customizable templates: Design Space includes a variety of pre-designed templates that you can customize to fit your needs.

Print then Cut feature: Design Space also offers a print then cut feature, which allows you to print designs onto a printable material and then cut them out using your Cricut machine.

Cloud-based software: Design Space is a cloud-based application, which means you can access your designs from anywhere with an internet connection. You can also share your designs with others or collaborate on projects with friends or family members.

Tips: Beginners should use customized templates in Cricut Design Space as this will save time and help you create more consistent and professional-looking projects.

Templates are pre-designed layouts that you can customize to fit your needs, and they are available for various project types, including cards, invitations, labels, and more.

(4) Manage your Crafting Materials:

Always avoid waste, and ensure that your materials are appropriately used. The design space helps to align the materials before cutting, so there'll be no waste.

There are times you'll have to reuse some of the materials. Materials like transfer tape can be reused. There are many other ways to reuse crafting materials.

Some leftover crafting materials, like vinyl; fabrics, can be reused in future projects. When working with intricate vinyl designs or lettering, use transfer paper.

If you can also measure and cut your materials very well before placing them on the mat, it will also help preserve them. Double-check your settings and make sure you do test work before cutting.

How to Create Your First Cricut Project:

After following the previously highlighted steps, here are the basic steps to create your first Cricut Project:

- **Open Design Space:** The first step is to open the Cricut Design Space in your computer or iPad. Ensure that you device is connected to the Cricut Explore 3.

- **Choose a project:** Once you're logged into Design Space, you can browse through various pre-made projects or create your own. To get started, select "***Project***" from the Design Space dashboard or click "***New Project***" to create your own.

- **Customize your project:** Depending on the project you've chosen, you can customize the colors, fonts, and other design elements. Use the tools in Design Space to adjust the design to your liking.

- **Prepare your material:** Before you can cut your design, you'll need to prepare your material. Load the material onto your cutting mat and adjust the settings in Design Space accordingly. You may need to adjust the blade depth and pressure settings depending on the material you're using.

- **Send your design to the machine:** Once your material is loaded and your settings are adjusted, you're ready to send your design to the machine. Click on "*Make It*" in Design Space.

- **Customize Print Settings:** Here, you will need to preview the print settings, customize the material for printing, the material size, and print copies. Click on "*Apply*" to start the cutting process.

- **Assemble your project:** Once the machine has finished cutting your design, you'll need to assemble it.

- Depending on the project, this may involve weeding the excess material, transferring the design to a different surface, or attaching different pieces together.

That's it! With these basic steps, you should be able to create your first Cricut Explore 3 project using Design Space. Have fun crafting!

NOTE: For a first-timer, you are bound to make a series of mistakes when crafting with design space and printing with the Cricut explore 3. Sometimes, it may be frustrating, and you will be annoyed. However, the key to overcoming frustration is managing your expectations and avoiding the perfectionist mentality.

CHAPTER SEVEN

Cricut Blades and Machine Tools

In this chapter, we will dive deep into the world of Cricut blades and machine tools. You'll learn about the different types of blades available for various materials and the importance of properly maintaining and replacing your blades.

We'll also explore the different machine tools available, such as scoring wheels and pens, and how they can elevate your projects to the next level.

Whether you're a seasoned Cricut user or just starting out, this chapter will provide you with valuable information and tips to help you make the most of your machine and tools. So let's get started with your Cricut.

Cricut Blades:

Cricut Explore Blades are the cutting tools used in Cricut Explore and Cricut Maker machines to cut various materials, such as paper, vinyl, fabric, and more. Different types of blades are available to cut different materials. Here is an example of the different Cricut blades;

(1) Premium Fine-Point Blade:

The Cricut Explore 3 Premium Fine-Point Blade is a cutting tool used in the Cricut Explore 3 and other Cricut machines to cut various materials with precision and accuracy.

This blade is a step up from the standard Fine-Point Blade, providing even better performance for more demanding projects. The Premium Fine-Point Blade features a smaller, more durable tip, allowing for cleaner cuts on intricate designs and smaller details.

This blade also has a longer lifespan compared to the

standard Fine-Point Blade, making it a more cost-effective option in the long run. One of the main advantages of the Premium Fine-Point Blade is its versatility. It can be used on a wide range of materials, including:

- Cardstock

- Vinyl

- Iron-on

- Posterboard

- Deluxe paper

- Foil and Infusible Ink

The Premium Fine-Point Blade can also be used with the Cricut Smart Materials, which allows for cutting without a cutting mat. This feature is particularly useful for larger projects and allows for continuous cutting without interruption.

Another advantage of the Premium Fine-Point Blade

is its compatibility with the Cricut Roll Holder. This accessory allows for easy cutting of long rolls of material, such as vinyl or iron-on, without the need for manual adjustment.

(2) Deep Point Blade:

The Cricut Explore 3 Deep Point Blade is a cutting tool that is designed to cut through thicker materials than the standard fine-point blade. This blade is compatible with the Cricut Explore 3 and Cricut Maker 3 machines.

The function of the Cricut Explore 3 Deep Point Blade is to cut through materials that are up to 2.4mm thick, including materials such as chipboard, foam board, leather, and more. It features a steeper blade angle and a longer blade, allowing it to cut through thicker materials easily.

The advantages of using the Cricut Explore 3 Deep Point Blade are numerous. For one, it allows you to cut through thicker materials, which opens up a whole new range of possibilities for your projects.

You can create 3D projects, custom gift boxes, and other unique items requiring thicker material. Additionally, the Deep Point Blade can save you time and effort by cutting through multiple layers of material in a single pass.

Some of the materials that can be used with the Cricut Explore 3 Deep Point Blade include:

- **Chipboard:** This material is ideal for creating sturdy 3D projects, such as boxes, frames, and other dimensional items.

- **Leather:** The Deep Point Blade can cut through leather to create custom accessories, such as belts, wallets, and bags.

- **Foam board:** This material is perfect for creating custom signs, posters, and other large-scale projects.

- **Balsa wood:** The Deep Point Blade can cut through balsa wood to create unique wooden ornaments, signs, and more.

(3) Bonded-Fabric Blade:

The Cricut Explore 3 Bonded-Fabric Blade is a cutting tool designed specifically for cutting fabrics without fraying or tearing. It's one of the blades available for use in the Cricut Explore 3 machine, a versatile cutting machine that can cut various materials with precision and ease.

The Bonded-Fabric Blade features a specially designed rotary cutting wheel that works in conjunction with the machine's Adaptive Tool System to apply the ideal amount of pressure and angle for each cut.

This helps to ensure clean, precise cuts every time without damaging the fabric or causing it to unravel. One of the advantages of using the Cricut Explore 3 Bonded-Fabric Blade is that it makes cutting fabrics incredibly easy and efficient.

Unlike traditional fabric scissors or rotary cutters, the Bonded-Fabric Blade allows you to cut fabrics with incredible speed and precision without worrying about frayed edges or uneven cuts.

It's also much safer than traditional cutting tools, as the machine's design ensures that your fingers are always kept away from the blade. The Cricut Explore 3 Bonded-Fabric Blade can be used on various materials, including cotton, felt, fleece, denim, and even leather.

It's perfect for cutting out shapes and patterns for quilting, sewing, and other fabric-based crafts. Additionally, because the blade is designed to work with bonded fabrics, it can easily cut through materials backed with fusible interfacing or stabilizer.

TIPS: *Deep-Point blades should be used only in Deep-Point blade housings, and Premium Fine-Point blades should be used only in the Premium Fine-Point blade housing.*

Machine Tools:

The Cricut machine tool allows you to cut and create various projects. These machine tools can be quickly and easily swapped out, depending on the type of material. Here are the machine tools that are available for use with the Cricut Explore 3;

(1) Foil Transfer Tool:

The Foil Transfer Tool is a specialized tool designed to add foil accents to various materials using the Cricut Explore 3 cutting machine. This tool allows you to create stunning designs with a metallic finish, making your projects look elegant and professional.

The Foil Transfer Tool uses a heated tip to transfer the foil onto the material. It comes with three interchangeable tips that can be used to create different line weights and designs.

The tool is easy to use, and the Cricut Design Space

software provides pre-made foil designs or the ability to create custom designs. Advantages of using the Cricut Explore 3 Foil Transfer Tool include:

- **Versatility:** The Foil Transfer Tool can be used on various materials, including cardstock, adhesive-backed paper, vinyl, and leather.

- **Precision:** The tool provides precise and accurate foil transfers, making it easy to create intricate designs.

- **Ease of use:** The tool is easy to install and use, and the Cricut Design Space software provides step-by-step instructions.

- **Customization:** The tool allows for customization so that you can create unique designs for your projects.

Materials that can be used with the Cricut Explore 3 Foil Transfer Tool include:

- **Cardstock:** This material is perfect for creating cards, invitations, and other paper crafts.

- **Adhesive-backed paper:** This material is ideal for creating labels and stickers.

- **Vinyl:** This material is great for adding foil accents to wall decals, phone cases, and other personalized items.

- **Leather:** This material can be used to create customized accessories like wallets, belts, and bracelets.

(2) Scoring Stylus:

Scoring Stylus is a tool designed to create fold lines in various materials using a Cricut Explore 3 machine. The scoring stylus is used to create precise creases and score lines that make it easy to fold your material accurately and cleanly.

The scoring stylus is compatible with a variety of materials, including paper, cardstock, vellum, and acetate. One of the key advantages of the Cricut Explore 3 Scoring Stylus is that it allows you to create intricate, complex designs with ease.

By scoring your material in advance, you can create precise folds and intricate shapes that would be difficult to achieve otherwise. This makes the scoring stylus an essential tool for creating 3D projects, such as pop-up cards and paper sculptures.

Another advantage of the scoring stylus is that it helps to prevent cracking and tearing in your material. When you fold paper or cardstock without a score line, it can be difficult to create a clean, straight fold without damaging the material. By using the scoring stylus to create a score line, you can fold your material with ease and without the risk of tearing or cracking.

(3) Roll Holder:

Roll Holder is an accessory for the Cricut Explore 3 cutting machine that allows users to easily and conveniently store and use multiple rolls of material simultaneously.

This roll holder is designed to clip onto the machine and can hold up to three rolls of material, allowing users to quickly switch between different colors or types of material without manually swapping them out.

One of the key advantages of the Cricut Explore 3 Roll Holder is that it can significantly increase efficiency and productivity for users who frequently work with multiple rolls of material.

Users can save time and streamline their workflow by eliminating the need to constantly swap out rolls, allowing them to complete projects more quickly and efficiently.

Additionally, the Roll Holder is designed to be versatile and can be used with a wide range of materials, including vinyl, iron-on, cardstock, paper, and more. This means that users can take advantage of the roll holder regardless of the type of project they are working on or the specific materials they are using.

The Roll Holder is also made from high-quality materials that are designed to be durable and long-lasting. This ensures that users can rely on the roll holder to perform reliably and consistently over time, even with frequent use.

How to Care For Cricut Blades and Machine Tools:

Taking good care of your Cricut blades and machine tools is essential for ensuring they stay in good working condition and last as long as possible. Here are some tips for caring for your Cricut blades and machine tools:

Keep your blades and machine tools clean: After each use, it's essential to clean your blades and machine tools. Use a soft-bristled brush to remove any debris or dust that may have accumulated on them. If there's any stubborn residue, you can use a damp cloth or a mild cleaning solution.

Use a cutting mat: Using a cutting mat when cutting materials with your Cricut machine will help protect your blades from dulling quickly. Make sure to clean the cutting mat regularly, as well, to prevent debris buildup.

Use the correct blade for the job: Using the correct blade for the material you're cutting will not only ensure that you get the best results but also help prevent unnecessary wear and tear on your blades.

Store your blades properly: When not in use, store your blades in their original packaging or in a dedicated blade storage container to protect them from damage.

Keep your machine clean: Regularly clean your Cricut machine to prevent any buildup of debris or dust that could damage the machine's moving parts or cause it to malfunction.

Don't force your machine or blades: If you encounter any resistance or difficulty when cutting, don't force your machine or blades. Instead, stop the machine and check to see if there's anything obstructing the blades or if the blade needs replacing.

By following these tips, you can help ensure that your Cricut blades and machine tools stay in good working condition for as long as possible.

CHAPTER EIGHT

Cricut Materials

In this chapter, we will explore the various materials that can be used with a Cricut machine. Each material has its own unique properties and cutting requirements, and understanding these is essential for achieving the best results.

We will cover everything from basic cardstock to more complex materials like leather and wood, providing step-by-step instructions and tips for getting the most out of each material.

Vinyl:

There are several types of vinyl materials that can be used with Cricut Explore 3. Here are the most common types and their recommended uses:

- **Permanent Vinyl:** This type of vinyl is great for projects that will be used outdoors or need to be washed frequently, as it is waterproof and durable. It can be used on various surfaces, such as metal, glass, and plastic. Use the Fine Point Blade for cutting Permanent vinyl.

- **Removable Vinyl:** As the name suggests, this type of vinyl can be removed easily without leaving any residue behind. It is best used for temporary projects like decals, labels, and wall art. Use the Fine Point Blade for cutting Removable Vinyl.

- **Heat Transfer Vinyl (HTV):** HTV is used

to create custom designs on fabric items such as t-shirts, bags, and hats. It comes in various colors and finishes, like glitter and metallic. Use the Fine Point Blade for cutting HTV.

- **Dry Erase Vinyl:** This vinyl has a special coating that allows it to be written on with dry-erase markers and then wiped clean. It is perfect for creating reusable calendars, charts, and signs. Use the Fine Point Blade for cutting Dry Erase Vinyl.

- **Adhesive Foil:** Adhesive foil has a metallic or holographic finish that adds a touch of glam to any project. It is perfect for adding accents to home decor or paper crafts. Use the Fine Point Blade for cutting Adhesive Foil.

When selecting the appropriate blade for each type of vinyl material, it is recommended to use the Fine Point Blade for most materials.

Paper:

Cricut Explore 3 can cut various types of paper materials. Here are some of the most common ones and when to use them:

- **Cardstock:** Cardstock is a thick paper material that is perfect for creating cards, invitations, and other paper crafts. It comes in various weights and textures, and some are even glitter or metallic. Use a fine-point blade when cutting cardstock.

- **Adhesive-backed paper:** Adhesive-backed paper is a paper material with a sticky backing that is perfect for creating stickers and labels. It comes in various colors and finishes, such as matte or glossy. Use a fine-point blade when cutting adhesive-backed paper.

- **Vellum:** Vellum is a translucent paper material

that is perfect for creating delicate designs or lay-ering. It comes in various weights and textures. Use a fine-point blade when cutting vellum.

In general, a fine-point blade is suitable for cutting most paper materials. However, use a deep-point blade for thicker materials, such as cardstock to ensure a clean cut.

Leather:

There are different types of leather materials that can be used with the Cricut Explore 3, each with its unique characteristics and recommended uses. Here are some of the most common types of leather materials and their recommended uses, as well as the Cricut blades to use:

- **Genuine Leather:** This is the real deal, made from the hide of an animal. It is durable, long-lasting, and comes in various colors and textures. It's best used for projects that require a sturdy material, such as bags, wallets, and belts.

Use the Cricut Deep Cut Blade for this type of leather.

- **Faux Leather:** Also known as synthetic leather, this is a man-made material that imitates the look and feel of real leather. It's often less expensive than the genuine leather and comes in various colors and textures. It's best used for projects that don't require the durability of real leather, such as earrings, hair accessories, and home decor. Use the Cricut Fine Point Blade for this type of leather.

- **Suede:** This is a type of leather that has a napped surface, giving it a soft, velvety texture. It's often used for clothing, shoes, and home decor. Suede can be trickier to work with than other types of leather because of its delicate texture, but it's still possible to cut with the Cricut Explore 3. Use the Cricut Deep Cut Blade for suede.

- **Tooling Leather:** This is a thick, stiff leather that's often used for carving and tooling. It's typically used for creating belts, saddles, and other items that require a lot of detail work. Tooling leather can be cut with the Cricut Explore 3, but it's best to use the Cricut Deep Cut Blade and multiple passes to ensure a clean cut.

- **Garment Leather:** This is a thin, supple leather that's often used for clothing and accessories. It's typically softer and more flexible than other types of leather, making it easier to work with. Use the Cricut Fine Point Blade for this type of leather.

The recommended Cricut blades to use depend on the thickness and texture of the leather. The Deep Cut Blade is best for thick or tough leather, while the Fine Point Blade is ideal for thinner or more delicate materials.

Nylon:

Nylon is a synthetic material used for various crafting and sewing projects. When it comes to using nylon with a Cricut Explore 3 cutting machine, there are several different types of nylon materials to choose from, each with its own unique characteristics and recommended uses.

- **Nylon Fabric:** This type of nylon is commonly used in sewing projects, such as bags, outdoor gear, and clothing. It is typically thin and light-weight, making it easy to work with. The recommended blade to use with nylon fabric is the Fine-Point Blade.

- **Nylon Mesh:** This type of nylon is commonly used in crafting projects, such as creating stencils or decorative accents. It is typically semi-transparent and has a porous texture. The recommended blade to use with nylon mesh is the Fine-Point Blade.

- **Nylon Sticker Sheets:** This type of nylon is typically used for creating custom decals or stickers. It has a self-adhesive backing that allows it to be easily applied to a variety of surfaces. The recommended blade to use with nylon sticker sheets is the Fine-Point Blade.

- **Nylon Webbing:** This type of nylon is commonly used in outdoor gear, such as backpacks and harnesses. It is typically thicker and more durable than nylon fabric. The recommended blade to use with nylon webbing is the Deep-Point Blade.

In general, when working with nylon materials on a Cricut Explore 3, it is important to adjust the settings to the appropriate material type and thickness. This will ensure that the machine cuts the material accurately and cleanly.

Fabric:

There are different types of fabric materials that you can use with the Cricut Explore 3, and they are as follows:

- **Cotton:** Cotton is a popular fabric material that is widely used for making clothes, bags, and home decor items. You can use the Fine-Point Blade to cut cotton fabrics with the Cricut Explore 3.

- **Felt:** Felt is a soft and versatile fabric material that is often used for crafting and sewing projects. You can use the Fine-Point Blade to cut felt with the Cricut Explore 3.

- **Denim:** Denim is a sturdy fabric material that is often used for making jeans, jackets, and other clothing items. You can use the Fine-Point Blade to cut denim with the Cricut Explore 3.

- **Canvas:** Canvas is a heavy-duty fabric material

that is often used for making bags, shoes, and other accessories. You can use the Fine-Point Blade to cut canvas with the Cricut Explore 3.

- **Burlap:** Burlap is a coarse and durable fabric material that is often used for making home decor items, such as curtains and table runners. You can use the Fine-Point Blade to cut burlap with the Cricut Explore.

It's important to note that the recommended blade for each type of fabric material may vary depending on the thickness and density of the fabric. Before cutting any fabric material, it's recommended to perform a test cut on a small piece of fabric to determine the appropriate settings for the material and blade.

How to Set Up Cricut Material for Cutting:

Most cutting mats come in two different types of measurements: centimeters and inches. They also come with angled and grid lines, which are useful if you want to cut your lines to match on both sides. So, set up your cutting on a flat table and place your fabric on it. Place one hand on the fabric to hold it in place, and use your other hand to do the cutting.

How to Care for your Cricut Materials:

Proper care of your Cricut materials is important to ensure their longevity and to produce high-quality results. Here are ten tips on how to care for your Cricut materials:

- **Store materials in a cool, dry place:** Moisture

can damage some Cricut materials, so it is important to store them in a dry place away from direct sunlight or heat.

- **Keep materials flat:** Cricut materials, such as vinyl and iron-on, can become warped if stored improperly. Keep them flat and in their original packaging to prevent bending or creasing.

- **Keep materials clean:** Before cutting, make sure your materials are clean and free of debris. Use a lint roller or soft cloth to remove any dust or debris from your materials.

- **Use the correct blade:** Different Cricut materials require different blades to cut properly. Make sure to use the correct blade for your material to prevent damage to the material or the machine.

- **Adjust pressure settings:** Adjust the pressure settings on your Cricut machine to match the material you are cutting. This will help prevent the material from tearing or becoming damaged.

- **Use transfer tape:** When transferring vinyl or iron-on designs, use transfer tape to prevent the design from shifting or becoming misaligned.

- **Avoid overcutting:** Overcutting can damage your Cricut mat and your blade. Make sure to set your blade depth correctly and avoid cutting too deeply into your mat.

- **Clean your mat:** Clean your Cricut mat regularly to prevent debris and residue from building up. Use a scraper tool or lint roller to remove any debris.

- **Store mats flat:** After use, store your Cricut mat flat to prevent it from warping or becoming damaged.

- **Use a protective cover:** Consider using a protective cover for your Cricut machine to prevent dust or debris from accumulating on the machine and to protect it from scratches.

CHAPTER NINE

Cricut Accessories and Tools

There are numerous Cricut accessories that can aid your crafting process. In this chapter, you'll be learning extensively about the different Cricut accessories. So, let get started!!

These Cricut accessories and tools can help you create more efficiently craft, achieve precise results, and expand your creative possibilities. Here are some of the most popular Cricut accessories and tools:

Cutting Mats:

Cricut cutting mats come in a variety of sizes and degrees of stickiness. Depending on your material, you will want less or more stickiness on your mat.

The Cricut Weeder:

The weeder tool, which looks similar to a dental pick, is used for removing negative space from a vinyl project. This weeder tool is a must when doing any project that involves vinyl.

Trying to get rid of access vinyl is nearly only possible with a weeder, especially with glitter iron-on materials. A weeder is a useful tool for any project using adhesives. Instead of picking up the adhesive with your fingertips, use the weeder tool and keep your fingers sticky.

The Cricut Scraper:

The Cricut Scraper tool is essential (and a lifesaver!) when you need to rid your cutting mat of excess negative bits. This tool typically works best with paper, such as cardstock, but other materials can easily be scraped up as well.

Use the mat's flexibility to your advantage as you scrap the bits off the mat to ensure you are not scraping up the adhesive on the mat as well. You can also use the Cricut Scraper as a scoreline holder, which allows you to fold over the scoreline with a nice crisp edge.

It can also be used as a burnishing tool for Cricut transfer tape, as it will allow seamless separation of the transfer tape from the backing.

The Cricut Spatula:

A spatula is a must-have tool for a crafter who works with many papers. Pulling the paper off of a Cricut cut mat can result in a lot of tearing and paper curling if you are not diligent and mindful when removing it.

The spatula is thinly designed to slip right under the paper, allowing you to carefully ease it off the mat. Be sure to clean it often, as it is likely to get the adhesive built upon it after multiple uses.

The Cricut Tweezers:

Projects that involve a lot of embellishments will require a pair of tweezers. The Cricut tweezers can be awkward to use at first, as they function directly opposite to what we are used to with traditional tweezers.

They need to be squeezed to open them instead of squeezing them to shut. Ultimately, you will begin to realize the genius behind this design because you will be able to pick something up and release pressure on it.

The Cricut tweezers will hold pressure on the object and you'll be saved from continuously dropping small pieces that may lead to cramps on your hands.

The Cricut Scissors:

Using the right scissors for a job can make a world of difference. The Cricut Scissors are made from stainless steel to ensure they will stick around for many jobs before getting dull.

The scissors come with a micro-tip blade, so finer details in smaller areas are easier and clean right down to a point.

The Cricut Scoring Tool:

If you want to do projects that involve a scoring line, such as folding cards in half or making 3D boxes, you should invest in a Cricut Scoring tool.

You can insert this tool into the second tool holder, or accessory clamp, into the Cricut, Explore itself, and the Cricut will use it to make score lines wherever the design dictates.

They will need to be present in the Cricut Design Space file for the machine to recognize the scoreline is needed in the project.

The basic tool kit Cricut sold does not have a scoring tool. You will need to purchase this separately. If you plan to work with many paper projects, this is an excellent tool to invest in.

The Cricut Easy press:

If you begin to venture into iron-on projects and want to upgrade from a traditional iron and ironing board, the Cricut Easypress is the right way to go. It will make projects so much easier than using a traditional iron.

The Cricut Easypress is known to help keep designed adhered for longer, essentially no more peeling of designs after one or two uses and washes.

The Easypress also takes all of the guesswork out of the right amount of contact time and temperature.

The Cricut Brightpad:

Brightpad reduces eyestrain while making crafting easier. It is designed to illuminate fine lines for tracing, cut lines for weeding, and so much more! It is thin and lightweight, which allows for durable transportation.

BrightPad makes crafting more enjoyable with its adjustable, evenly lit surface. The bright LED lights can be adjusted depending on the workspace. The only downfall to this accessory is that it must be plugged in a while used. It does not contain a rechargeable battery.

The Cricut Cuttlebug Machine:

The Cricut Cuttlebug is an embossing and dies-cutting machine that offers portability and versatility in cutting and embossing. This machine gives professional-looking results with clean, crisp, and deep embosses.

CHAPTER TEN

What Never to Do with Cricut Explore 3?

Cricut Design Space is a web-based software program developed by Cricut that allows users to design and create projects to be used with Cricut cutting machines. It offers a wide variety of features, including the ability to create and edit designs, import and customize images, and choose from various pre-designed projects and patterns.

Cricut Design Space is accessible through a web browser and can be used on both Windows and Mac operating systems. It also has a mobile app for iOS and Android devices, allowing users to design on-the-go.

Get Started with Design Space:

After installing the software on your device, you can use it online and offline to create and layout designs. The software offers you a wide range of art and fonts, or you can choose from pre-designed projects. Once you have finished setting up, you can access the main software, and the first thing you will see is the home screen page.

The Cricut Design Space homepage is the gateway to your creative crafting journey with Cricut. When you first launch Design Space, you'll be greeted with an inviting and user-friendly interface designed to inspire and empower you to create.

Homepage:

Here's what you can expect when you open the Cricut Design Space app on your computer:

Discover: In this section, you'll be greeted with various project ideas, trending designs, and seasonal inspirations. Explore a rotating carousel of featured projects and discover new creative possibilities to ignite your imagination.

My Stuff: This section allows you to access all your saved projects, uploaded images, and stored designs. This personalized space allows you to manage and organize your completed projects easily and works in progress.

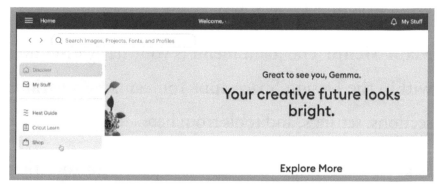

Heat Guide: This section is a valuable resource that provides temperature and time settings for heat transfer materials. Whether working with iron-on or infusible ink, this guide ensures that you achieve professional and long-lasting results with your Cricut Machine.

Cricut Learn: In this section, you'll find a wealth of tutorials, guides, and how-to articles that cater to crafters of all levels. Whether you're a beginner or a seasoned pro, these educational resources will help you master the Cricut Machine and enhance your crafting skills.

Shop: This section offers access to the Cricut Design Space Store, where you can browse and purchase a vast selection of premium images, fonts, and ready-to-make projects. You can also explore materials, tools, and accessories to complement your crafting endeavors.

Main Menu: The main menu is your navigation hub within the Design Space app. You can access various sections, settings, and tools from here.

Search Bar: The search bar is a powerful tool that lets you quickly find specific projects, images, fonts, and materials within the Design Space library. Whether you're looking for a particular design or a project related to a specific theme, the search bar simplifies discovering inspiration.

My Stuf: This section is your personalized space within

the app. You can access your uploaded images, projects, and saved designs here. It's a convenient way to organize and keep track of your creative work, ensuring that your projects are always at your fingertips.

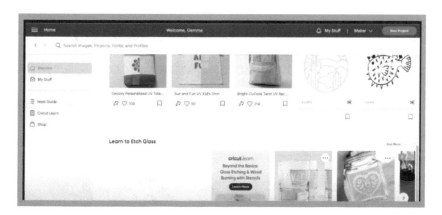

Maker: The Maker section contains information and settings related to your Cricut Maker 3 cutting machine. You can manage machine-specific settings, connect to your Maker via Bluetooth or USB, and view any updates or notifications relevant to your machine.

New Project: When you are ready to start a new crafting adventure, click on the New Project, and it will open up a blank canvas where you can let your creativity flow. This is where you'll design, customize, and edit your projects, selecting the materials, shapes, and sizes that suit your vision.

Main Menu:

The main menu is your navigation hub within the Design Space app. You can access various sections, settings, and tools from here. Here is a summary of how to use the main menu:

When click on the three lines to pull down the menu, you'll see a long line of things listed, but you'll only need to focus on a few of them.

My Profile: At the top of the menu are your initials inside a circle by your name and a **"View Profile."** When you click on the view profile, you will be redirected to your Profile Page.

In my profile section, select **"Edit Profile"** icon and you will be directed to the Edit Profile menu. Here, you can upload your profile picture by clicking on the big circle and following the onscreen prompts.

You can also write a short bio about yourself. Ensure to craft a compelling bio that showcases your skill. When you upload your craft to Cricut community, people can read your profile.

Canvas: The Canvas option takes you to the design canvas, where you can create and edit your projects. In subsequent chapters, we shall explain how to use Cricut Design Space canvas.

New Product Setup: If you have a new Cricut machine or accessory, the New Product Setup option guides you through the process of setting up your device and ensuring it's ready for crafting.

Calibration: Calibration is essential for precise cutting. This option helps you calibrate your Cricut machine, ensuring accurate cuts on various materials.

Manage Custom Material: If you work with unique or specialized materials, the Manage Custom Material option allows you to add, edit, or delete custom material settings for your projects.

Update Firmware: Firmware updates are important for keeping your Cricut machine running smoothly and efficiently. This option allows you to check for and install the latest firmware updates for your device.

Account Details: The Account Details section provides an overview of your Cricut account, including your subscription status, billing information, and membership details.

Link Cartridge: If you own physical cartridges for older Cricut machines, the Link Cartridge option allows you to link them to your Cricut Design Space account for digital access to their content.

Cricut Access: Cricut Access is a subscription service that provides access to a vast library of premium images, fonts, and projects. This option allows you to manage your Cricut Access subscription.

Settings: The Settings section lets you customize your Cricut Design Space preferences, such as General settings, Canvas, Load Type, and Notification settings.

Legal: The Legal option provides access to important legal information, terms of use, and privacy policies related to using Cricut Design Space.

What's New: This option keeps you informed about the latest updates, features, and enhancements to Cricut Design Space.

CHAPTER ELEVEN

Design Space

Cricut Design Space is a web-based software program developed by Cricut that allows users to design and create projects to be used with Cricut cutting machines. It offers a wide variety of features, including the ability to create and edit designs, import and customize images, and choose from various pre-designed projects and patterns.

Cricut Design Space is accessible through a web browser and can be used on both Windows and Mac operating systems. It also has a mobile app for iOS and Android devices, allowing users to design on-the-go.

Get Started with Design Space:

After installing the software on your device, you can use it online and offline to create and layout designs. The software offers you a wide range of art and fonts, or you can choose from pre-designed projects. Once you have finished setting up, you can access the main software, and the first thing you will see is the home screen page.

The Cricut Design Space homepage is the gateway to your creative crafting journey with Cricut. When you first launch Design Space, you'll be greeted with an inviting and user-friendly interface designed to inspire and empower you to create.

Homepage:

Here's what you can expect when you open the Cricut Design Space app on your computer:

Discover: In this section, you'll be greeted with various project ideas, trending designs, and seasonal inspirations. Explore a rotating carousel of featured projects and discover new creative possibilities to ignite your imagination.

My Stuff: This section allows you to access all your saved projects, uploaded images, and stored designs. This personalized space allows you to manage and organize your completed projects easily and works in progress.

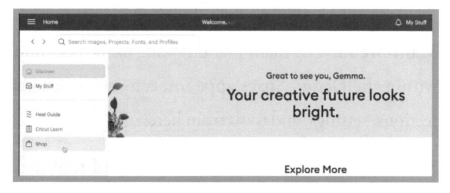

Heat Guide: This section is a valuable resource that provides temperature and time settings for heat transfer materials. Whether working with iron-on or infusible ink, this guide ensures that you achieve professional and long-lasting results with your Cricut Machine.

Cricut Learn: In this section, you'll find a wealth of tutorials, guides, and how-to articles that cater to crafters of all levels. Whether you're a beginner or a seasoned pro, these educational resources will help you master the Cricut Machine and enhance your crafting skills.

Shop: This section offers access to the Cricut Design Space Store, where you can browse and purchase a vast selection of premium images, fonts, and ready-to-make projects. You can also explore materials, tools, and accessories to complement your crafting endeavors.

Main Menu: The main menu is your navigation hub within the Design Space app. You can access various sections, settings, and tools from here.

Search Bar: The search bar is a powerful tool that lets you quickly find specific projects, images, fonts, and materials within the Design Space library. Whether you're looking for a particular design or a project related to a specific theme, the search bar simplifies discovering inspiration.

My Stuf: This section is your personalized space within

the app. You can access your uploaded images, projects, and saved designs here. It's a convenient way to organize and keep track of your creative work, ensuring that your projects are always at your fingertips.

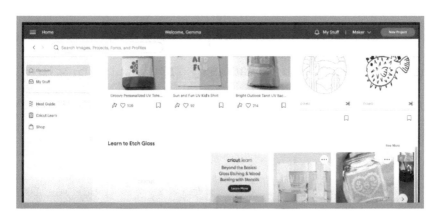

Maker: The Maker section contains information and settings related to your Cricut Maker 3 cutting machine. You can manage machine-specific settings, connect to your Maker via Bluetooth or USB, and view any updates or notifications relevant to your machine.

New Project: When you are ready to start a new crafting adventure, click on the New Project, and it will open up a blank canvas where you can let your creativity flow. This is where you'll design, customize, and edit your projects, selecting the materials, shapes, and sizes that suit your vision.

Main Menu:

The main menu is your navigation hub within the Design Space app. You can access various sections, settings, and tools from here. Here is a summary of how to use the main menu:

When click on the three lines to pull down the menu, you'll see a long line of things listed, but you'll only need to focus on a few of them.

My Profile: At the top of the menu are your initials inside a circle by your name and a **"View Profile."** When you click on the view profile, you will be redirected to your Profile Page.

In my profile section, select **"Edit Profile"** icon and you will be directed to the Edit Profile menu. Here, you can upload your profile picture by clicking on the big circle and following the onscreen prompts.

You can also write a short bio about yourself. Ensure to craft a compelling bio that showcases your skill. When you upload your craft to Cricut community, people can read your profile.

Canvas: The Canvas option takes you to the design canvas, where you can create and edit your projects. In subsequent chapters, we shall explain how to use Cricut Design Space canvas.

New Product Setup: If you have a new Cricut machine or accessory, the New Product Setup option guides you through the process of setting up your device and ensuring it's ready for crafting.

Calibration: Calibration is essential for precise cutting. This option helps you calibrate your Cricut machine, ensuring accurate cuts on various materials.

Manage Custom Material: If you work with unique or specialized materials, the Manage Custom Material option allows you to add, edit, or delete custom material settings for your projects.

Update Firmware: Firmware updates are important for keeping your Cricut machine running smoothly and efficiently. This option allows you to check for and install the latest firmware updates for your device.

Account Details: The Account Details section provides an overview of your Cricut account, including your subscription status, billing information, and membership details.

Link Cartridge: If you own physical cartridges for older Cricut machines, the Link Cartridge option allows you to link them to your Cricut Design Space account for digital access to their content.

Cricut Access: Cricut Access is a subscription service that provides access to a vast library of premium images, fonts, and projects. This option allows you to manage your Cricut Access subscription.

Settings: The Settings section lets you customize your Cricut Design Space preferences, such as General settings, Canvas, Load Type, and Notification settings.

Legal: The Legal option provides access to important legal information, terms of use, and privacy policies related to using Cricut Design Space.

What's New: This option keeps you informed about the latest updates, features, and enhancements to Cricut Design Space.

CHAPTER TWELVE

Design Space Canvas

Imagine the Design Space canvas as your own creative playground, where you can turn your ideas into stunning designs. On this platform, you can create new projects, add images and text to your existing work, and perfect them until they meet your expectations.

The Canvas:

The software's main work area is called the canvas. At first, it might seem confusing and too much to handle, but the more you use it, the easier it will become to understand the various icons, buttons, and options on the screen.

Additionally, you can use this book as a helpful guide to assist you in your journey. To help you understand better, I've divided the canvas screen into different sections:

Canvas Header:

The Cricut Design Space Canvas Header is the top section of the design canvas interface in Cricut Design Space. It plays a crucial role in providing important tools, options, and settings for creating and customizing your projects. Here's what you can expect to find in the Cricut Design Space Canvas Header:

Menu: This is simple to figure out, and it is the same as the Main menu button on the Homepage of Design Space. As explained earlier, the main menu is your navigation hub within the Design Space app.

You can access various sections, settings, and tools from here, allowing you to move between different aspects of your crafting experience seamlessly.

Title: The project title area displays the name of your current project. You can click on it to rename your project or add a description.

If you're working on more than one project at a time, which I don't recommend, then switching back and forth would become very frustrating if the title wasn't displayed.

My Projects: This button works exactly like the "My Projects" button on the Homepage.

It is important to note that if you click this part of the Header without saving your project first, you will lose your recent changes.

Save: The save button is the most important part of the Header, as it saves and updates your Design Space's recent changes.

Explore: This section changes depending on the machine you're sending your project to. When you click the down arrow, it gives you a Dropbox with the machines listed.

Make It: Once you finish your creation, it's time to print it (if there's any printing involved) and cut it. This is what the "**Make It**" button is for. It's the only one that actually looks like a button.

The Cricut Design Space Canvas Header provides easy access to essential tools and options for designing and refining your projects. It ensures a seamless and user-friendly experience, making bringing your creative visions to life easier than ever.

Design Panel:

On the right side, you'll see the design panel. The design panel of Design Space is a prominent and essential element of the software's interface. It offers a range of tools, features, and options that facilitate the design and customization process. Here's an overview of the components typically found in the left panel:

New:

On the left panel, the first option (New) is to start a new project. Clicking it will give you an empty canvas.

If you're already working on a project and click "**New**," a pop-up will ask if you want to save your current work.

Template:

To access templates for your design, click on the second tool on the left panel of your canvas. This will bring up a screen with numerous templates that can help you visualize how your design will appear on a surface.

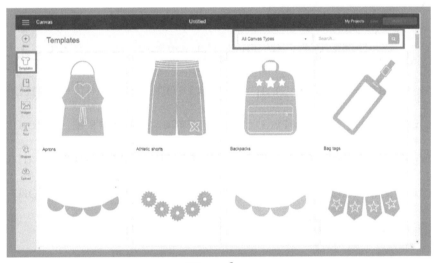

Template

You can select a template that matches what you want to create and use it as a guide to developing your own design. For example, if you want to add text to your shirt, you can select the shirt template, adjust the size and dimensions, and type in the text.

Once you have added your text, place it where you want it to be on the shirt.

Template Edit bar: After you've selected the template your Canvas will automatically zoom out to provide you with a complete view of the template. The Template Edit bar will appear at the top of the canvas offering you various customization options.

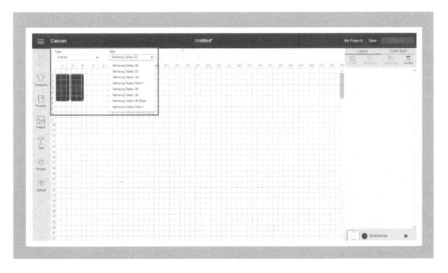

In the Template Edit bar you can find the **Type** and **Size** options allowing you to choose the template version that closely matches the item you intend to use.

Some templates also provide a "**Custom**" option in the Size panel enabling you to manually input specific dimensions. To design with the template effectively feel free to zoom in on the Canvas as required for precise adjustments and creative detailing.

It is important to note that you can modify the color of your template, and here is how to go about the process:

- The first step is to select (click on it) the template to reveal the Layers Panel at the top bar.

- Locate the **template color** swatch at the top of the Layers panel and click on it.

- A color options panel will appear, presenting various choices to customize your template's color.

- You can select from the existing project colors or choose one from the Basic colors palette.

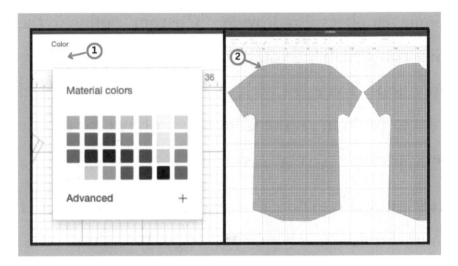

As you select, observe how the template on Canvas automatically updates to showcase your chosen color.

TIP: Although the templates cannot be saved or cut out, they are a great tool to help you visualize and set up the size, dimension, space, and other properties of your design.

Projects:

Fortunately, not only are the projects incredibly user-friendly, but they also unveil a plethora of delightful opportunities for Cricut crafting adventures, ensuring an enjoyable and exciting journey throughout.

With these projects at your disposal, you'll discover a world of creative possibilities, elevating the fun and fulfillment of your crafting experience to new heights.

Projects provides you with a various of design projects that are already created for you. This means that you don't have to be an expert in design to create a stunning design.

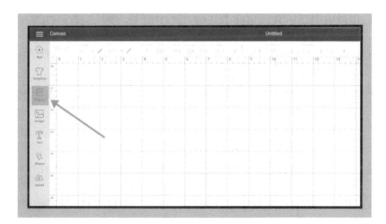

To access pre-designed projects, click on the 'Project' icon at the left side bar.

From there, you can scroll through and select any design you prefer. On the "All Projects" page, you can effortlessly discover projects within Design Space by using the search bar in the top right corner.

Alternatively, you can filter projects by category using the convenient dropdown menu. To search, enter a keyword into the search bar and click the magnifying glass icon.

Note: It's important to know that not all projects are free. Some require a purchase, but you can access most projects as a Cricut access member. Look for the projects with an 'A' sign on a little green banner, as those are available with your subscription.

If you're new to this Design Space, I suggest you explore the available free projects. To find them, click the drop-down button at the top right of the Project screen.

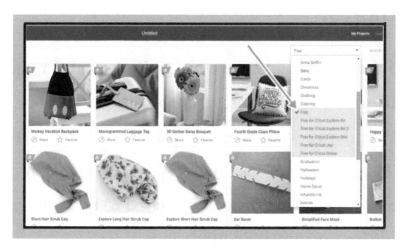

If you don't have a Cricut Access subscription, you can still make a one-time purchase of any project you're interested in. Once you've made the purchase, you'll be able to use the design as many times as you want, whenever you want.

If you click on the '**All Categories**' drop-down (top right corner of your screen), you will see a list of items to select from. They are simply inexhaustible.

Search Tip: For better search results, use singular words instead of plural. For example, searching for "**cat**" will give you more results than "**cats in a shirt**."

Images:

On the left panel, there is an option called '**Images**.' This tool helps add pictures to your design. For instance, if you want to create a tablecloth with a teddy bear image, you can click on the '**Image**' icon and browse through the images displayed to find a suitable teddy bear picture for your design.

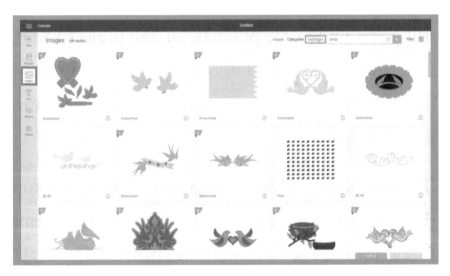

You can use the drop-down search button at the screen's

top right corner if you prefer a more specific search. Type in what you are looking for, such as a teddy bear, in the provided space. In the image search bar, you can browse, search, and filter images as needed. Unleash your imagination with the following options:

- **All Images:** Immerse yourself in a vast collection of featured images or conduct a specific search within the comprehensive Cricut library.

- **Categories:** Discover a diverse array of images by easily navigating through our thoughtfully curated image categories. Find the perfect fit for your project effortlessly.

- **Cartridges:** Embark on an alphabetical journey through over 400 Cricut cartridges (image sets) or conduct a swift search to locate a particular one.

It is possible to choose and add several images simultaneously to your project.

Text:

To add new text to the Canvas, click the Text icon on the left side of the design toolbar. The "Text" option will be highlighted, appearing in a text box.

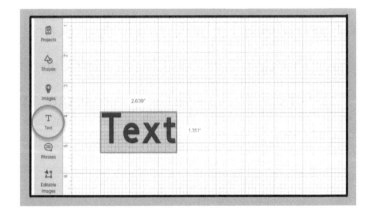

This indicates that you are in Edit mode, ready to customize the text. You can easily update the text by simply typing your desired content.

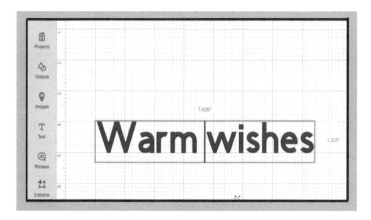

When you click outside the text box, you'll exit Edit mode. To edit a text, double-click on the text, and the text field will instantly enter Edit mode. Alternatively, right-click on your text and choose "Edit Text" from the menu to achieve the same result.

The second thing you will notice is that the top menu panel contains the Text edit menu, which is a function needed to edit your text. In the text edit panel, you can change the font of your text.

Once you have highlighted the desired letter(s), you

gain the ability to perform various actions, such as cutting, copying, and pasting. You can achieve this using either the options provided in the **Edit menu** or by right-clicking within the text box.

Font – Click on the font icon, and you will see several styles of font you can select from, including Cricut fonts and system fonts (fonts installed on your PC). You will also find other text editing attributes to set how you want your text to appear in your design.

In the font section, you can navigate through the available fonts section. The image below indicates the different sections of text font using indexes (A), the search field (B), or the filters (C) to discover the ideal font.

Font Style – You can select different font styles such as Bold, Italic, or Underline.

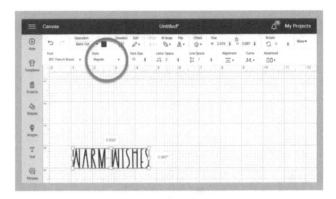

Font Size - You can increase or decrease the Font Size by using the input box. You can use the downward and upward pointing arrows to decrease or increase the font size.

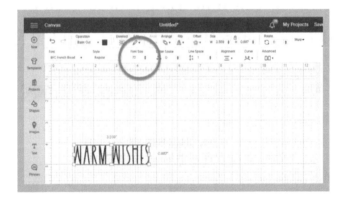

Rotate Text - To perform text rotation on Canvas; you have a couple of options at your disposal. Firstly, you can effortlessly rotate your text box by using any corner handle of the bounding box.

Alternatively, you can enter precise rotation values directly into the Rotate input field found in the Edit toolbar.

For a seamless rotation experience, use the bounding box corner handle. You can do this by hovering your cursor just outside the text until a curved arrow icon emerges.

Subsequently, click and drag in the desired direction to rotate the text to your preferred angle. This intuitive approach grants you full control over the rotation process, allowing you to achieve the perfect alignment for your design.

Resizing Text - You can adjust the size of the text by using the corner handle on the text bounding box.

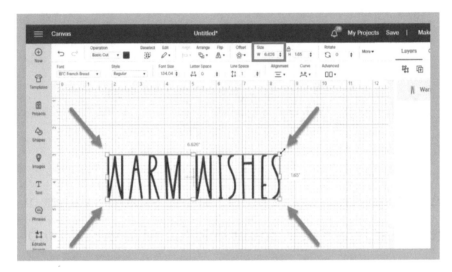

Alternatively, you can enter the precise sizing value in the Size input fields in the Edit toolbar.

Resizing the text box - To resize the box containing your text while keeping your chosen text size intact, click and drag the middle rectangular handles located on the bounding box. By default, the text is centered, and you can alter this arrangement.

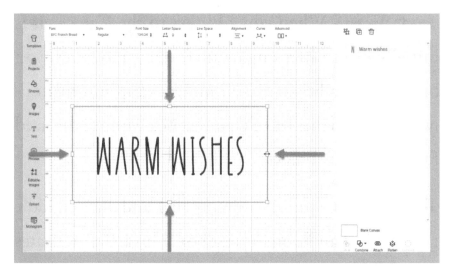

However, you have the flexibility to fine-tune the text's position within the text box using tools such as Alignment, Letter Space, and Line Space.

Text Wrap - When you add text to the Canvas, it is initially placed in a single-line format. However, you have the flexibility to make your text wrap automatically, adapting to the size of your text box without the need for manual line breaks.

To enable text wrapping, simply click and drag a middle rectangular handle on the text box. This action activates the Wrap mode, causing your text to flow to a new line as needed.

Consequently, you can effortlessly push a word to a new line or bring it back from the previous line to achieve your desired text layout.

If you wish to revert to the default single-line format,

you can exit the Wrap mode by selecting **"Wrap Off"** from the Alignment menu. This grants you full control over your text positioning and presentation, allowing you to create visually appealing designs with ease.

Curving Text - To curve your text, enter it into the text box and select your desired font and style. If necessary, use the Letter Space tool to adjust the spacing between letters. If you have multiple lines of text, it's best to enter each line in a separate text box or use the "Ungroup to Lines" tool to separate them.

Next, click on the Curve tool and allow Design Space to analyze your text size and spacing. Once complete, a slider and number field will appear. Slide the slider to the right to curve your text downwards.

Another useful text editing tool is the 'Isolate Layer' button. This is used for isolating a letter from a text, giving you the ability to edit that letter separately. So, you can choose to increase the size of a single letter, change the font style, rotate it, and so on.

The easiest way to isolate the letters in a text is to select the text on the canvas, right-click on the mouse, and select the '**Ungroup**' button from the drop-down.

Phrases:

Crafters can access free and premium quotes created by Cricut community members in the Phrases menu. This menu resembles the image menu but is specifically designed for writing.

This menu adds writing design to your project, from writing signs, labels, etc. You will be taken to the Phrase menu when you click on the **Phrase icon** on the design panel.

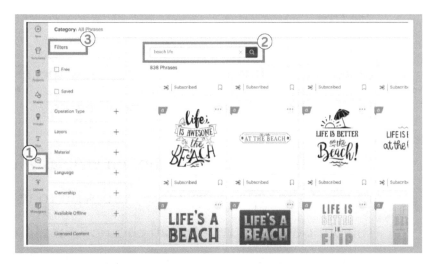

Search Bar: Within the Phrase menu, there is a search bar available for you to input the specific type of phrase bar available for you to input the specific type of phrase you require for your project. Once you have typed in your desired phrase and selected the search icon, an array of search results will be presented to you.

Filter: You will see the category option on the left-hand side of the Phrase menu. Here, you can narrow your search result just as with images. To refine your search, simply check the boxes that apply to your needs. Here are the category options available:

- **Free:** This option category helps you refine your search phrases by selecting only those that are free.

- **Saved:** This category allows you to view specific phrases that you have saved as bookmarks.

- **Operation:** This category option enables you to select the type of operation you wish to use the phrase for. Here, you can choose either Cut Only, Draw Only, Print then Cut, and Cut + Draw.

- **Layer:** Within the layer section, you have the option to select either Single Layer or Multi-Layer as the phrase to be used for your project.

- **Material:** Here, you can select the material that you want to use the phrases for. You can select from the options such as Chipboard, Infusable Ink, Iron-On, Leather, Paper/Cardstock, Sticker Paper, and Vinyl.

- **Language:** The language is where you can select the language of the phrase you want to use for your project.

- Other filter options include Ownership, Available Offline, and Licensed Content.

The Phrases tool in Cricut Design Space is a library of pre-designed phrases that you can use in your projects. The phrases are organized by category, so you can easily find what you're looking for. You can also filter the phrases by free, paid, or print and cut.

To use the Phrases tool, open Cricut Design Space and click on the Phrases button. The Phrases menu will appear. You can then use the filters to narrow down your search results. Once you've found a phrase you like, click on it to add it to your canvas.

You can resize, rotate, and position the phrase on your canvas as you see fit. You can also change the font, size, and color of the text. Once you're happy with the way the phrase looks, you can save your project and cut it out.

Shape:

The shape tool allows you to add shapes to your design. You can choose from a selection of different shapes to experiment with; square, circles, heart shape, star shape, triangle, etc.

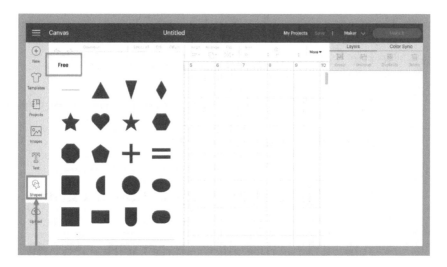

The exciting thing about working with shapes is the ability to customize them. You can add/change colors, add patterns, adjust the size, rotate them, etc. The possibilities are endless, as you will see later on in this book.

Once you've accessed the Shape feature, you can use it to create, modify, and arrange shapes in your design: To insert a shape into your canvas, simply click on the shape you want to use. It will appear in the center of your canvas.

The Shape section offers a range of pre-made shapes for your projects. These shapes are categorized for easy navigation, and you can filter them by free, paid, or print &

cut. To customize a shape in Cricut Design Space, you can use the following tools:

- **Weld:** This tool joins two or more shapes together into one new shape.

- **Slice:** This tool cuts out a section of a shape.

- **Align:** This tool aligns shapes with each other.

- **Transform:** This tool resizes, rotates, and mirrors shapes.

- **Fill:** This tool changes the color or pattern of a shape.

- **Linetype:** This tool changes the type of line used to outline a shape.

Shapes Tips:

Here are some tips for customizing shapes in Cricut Design Space:

- Use the Weld tool to join multiple shapes together to create new shapes.

- Use the Slice tool to cut out sections of shapes to create new designs.

- Use the Align tool to align shapes to each other to create symmetrical designs.

- Use the Transform tool to resize, rotate, and mirror shapes to create different looks.

- Use the Fill tool to change the color or pattern of a shape to create a variety of looks.

- Use the Linetype tool to change the type of line used to outline a shape to create different styles.

Editable Images:

Editable images is a section of the design panel where you can edit a portion of selected custom designs and customize it to whatever you want in your canvas.

In the Editable Images section, you'll find a collection of images that can be tailored to your liking with your own text. These images are ideal for designing unique gifts, cards, and other personal projects.

To use an editable image, simply click on the Editable Images button in the design panel. You can then browse through the library of images and find one that you like.

Once you've found an image, click on it to add it to your canvas.

After adding the image to your canvas will appear as a separate layer. To access the Layers panel, double-click on the layer. Once there, you'll notice that any editable text in the image is highlighted in blue. This indicates that the text can be easily edited.

To modify the text, just click on it and begin typing. You have the option to alter the font, size, color, and alignment of the text. Additionally, you can insert new text into the image. After you are satisfied with appearance of the text, you can save your project.

Editabke Images Tips:

Here are some tips for using editable images in Cricut Design Space:

Filter: Use the filters to narrow down your search results. You will see the category option on the left-hand side of the Editable Image menu. You can use this option to narrow your search result.

To refine your search, check the boxes that apply to your needs. Here are the category options available Free, Saved, Operation, Layer, Material, Language, etc.

Preview Images: Preview the image before you add it to your canvas. Previewing an image is a great way to make sure that the image is the size and shape you want and that it is aligned correctly on your canvas.

To preview an image, simply click on the "**Preview**" button in the top right corner of the image preview window. The image will then be displayed in a separate window, where you can see it at full size.

Layer Panel: Once you've found an image, click on it to add it to your canvas. The image will be added to your canvas as a separate layer. You can then double-click on the layer to open the Layers panel.

The Layer Panel is located on the right side of the Design Space window. Here, you'll see the text, images that are part of the editable images. Click on the editable text and start editing the text. You can change the font, size, color, and alignment of the text.

Editable images are a great way to personalize your projects. With so many images to choose from, you're sure to find the perfect one for your project.

Upload:

This is the second to last tool on the left panel of the canvas. When you click on it, it takes you to a screen where you can upload designs or images on your system to cut them with your Cricut. You could also get many pre-made designs from the internet, upload them into design space and cut them.

To use the Upload Section, click on the Upload button. The Upload menu will appear. You can then click on the **Upload Image**, **Upload Font**, or **Upload Project** button to upload your files.

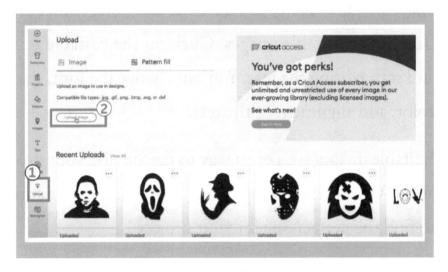

Once you've uploaded your files, they will be added to your Design Space library. You can then use them in your projects just like any other image, font, or project.

Here are some tips for using the Upload Section in Cricut Design Space:

- It is important to ensure that the images you use

are in a supported format when using Cricut Design Space. The supported file formats are PNG, JPEG, SVG, and DXF.

- To ensure compatibility, using fonts in either TTF or OTF format is important when working with Cricut Design Space.

- It's important to ensure that your projects are saved in a compatible format. Cricut Design Space can only accommodate SVG files.

- Preview your images and fonts before uploading them to ensure that your projects are of the right size and format. This way, you can make any necessary adjustments beforehand.

- It is important to give your files clear and specific names so that they can be easily located in the future.

Monogram:

The Monogram section is where you can access a variety of pre-made monograms for your projects. The monograms are arranged in categories, making it easy for you to find what you need. Additionally, you can filter them based on whether they are free, paid, or for print and cut purposes.

To access the Monogram section, click on the designated Monogram button at the bottom of the design panel. The Monogram menu will then appear, allowing you to filter and refine your search results.

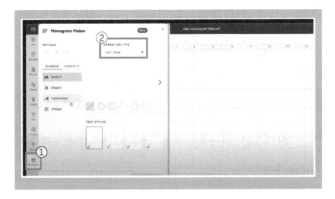

Once you've found a monogram that suits your needs, click on it to add it to your canvas. You can resize, rotate, and position the monogram on your canvas as you see fit. You can also change the font, size, and color of the text.

Once you're happy with the way the monogram looks, you can save your project and cut it out. Here are some tips for using the Monogram Section in Cricut Design Space:

- Use the filters to narrow down your search results.

- Preview the monogram before you add it to your canvas.

- Use the Weld tool to connect multiple letters together.

- Resize and position the monogram as you see fit.

- Change the font, size, and color of the text.

CHAPTER THIRTEEN

Editing Panel

To better understand the Top Bar in Design Space, it's important to define some key terminologies first. Please be aware that some of the terminology used in this guide are commonly used computer tools that should be easy to understand.

However, everyone's level of computer literacy may vary. Therefore, pardon me if you already know many of them. This has been done for the sake of those who do not know.

The Edit Bar, like the Text Bar, is only available when images or shapes are clicked and, therefore, editable.

Otherwise, the Edit Bar is unnecessarily wasted space. Here are the options that are available on the edit panel:

Undo/Redo:

This icon is used to reverse any change made to the layer or redo any previously taken undone action.

The undo/redo button is a handy tool in Cricut Design. These action buttons can be helpful if you make a mistake or if you want to experiment with different designs.

To use the undo/redo button, follow these steps:

1. To undo your last action, simply click on the left arrow button, which is the undo button.

2. To redo your last undone action, click on the redo button, which is indicated by a right arrow

symbol.

To perform undo and redo actions quickly, keyboard shortcuts can be used. If you are using a Mac, the undo shortcut is Command + Z, and the redo shortcut is Command + Shift + Z. If you are using a PC, the undo shortcut is Ctrl + Z, and the redo shortcut is Ctrl + Shift + Z.

Linetype:

This icon indicates how the machine will interact with the material on the mat, such as cut, draw, and score, on your material.

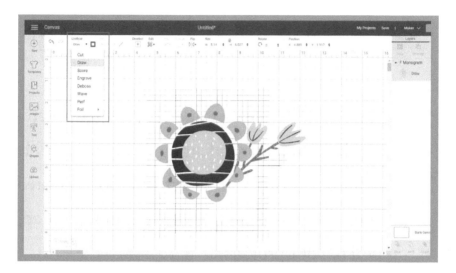

- **Draw:** The Draw line type utilizes a Cricut pen instead of a blade. It instructs the machine to draw along the designated path, adding decorative elements, handwritten text, or intricate patterns to your project.

- **Score:** The Score line type creates indentations or creases on your material without cutting through it completely. It is typically used for folding lines in projects such as cards, boxes, or other items that require clean and precise folds.

- **Engrave:** The Engrave line type is designed for

engraving, allowing you to create engraved designs or patterns on compatible materials.

- **Deboss:** The Deboss line type is used to create depressions or indentations on compatible materials, giving your designs a raised, textured effect. Debossing adds dimension and tactile appeal to your projects.

- **Wave:** The Wave line type, also known as the wavy line, creates a decorative wavy pattern along the designated path. It adds a fluid and dynamic element to your designs, enhancing the overall visual appeal with its flowing and undulating effect.

- **Perf:** The Perf line type, short for perforation, creates a series of small, evenly spaced holes along the designated path. It allows for easy tearing or separation of sections in projects like tear-away cards, or detachable elements.

- **Foil:** The Foil line type is specific to certain Cricut machines and tools designed for foiling. It enables you to add metallic or decorative foils to your designs, creating eye-catching accents or patterns on compatible materials.

These line types in Cricut Design Space offer a range of capabilities, allowing you to choose the appropriate method to achieve the desired outcome in your projects.

Linetype Swatch:

When creating a layer, you can choose additional attributes to use. The options available depend on the type of line chosen (cut, draw, or score).

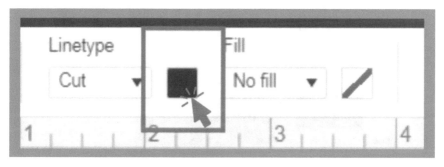

(1) **Cut Attributes:** These are the available attributes

that will show up when the '**Cut**' linetype is selected. The options available for cut attributes are;

- **Material colors:** To match project colors effortlessly, simply select your preferred shade from the Material colors palette. Once selected, a checkmark will appear in the color swatch for the chosen layer.

- **Advanced:** To choose a color, you can slide the bar in the custom color picker or manually enter the hexadecimal code of your desired color.

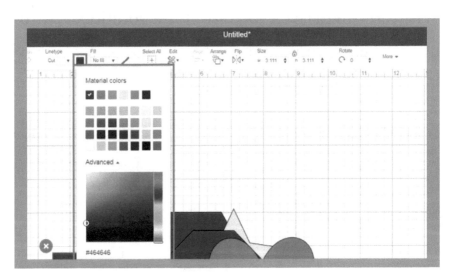

(2) **Draw Attributes:** When you choose the '**Draw**'

linetype, you will see these attributes available. To use a Cricut pen, select it from the drop-down menu. The list of available colors will vary based on the type of pen you choose.

Fill:

This is used to fill the image layers for printing with the chosen color or pattern.

- **No Fill:** This is used to cut the layer without filling the image layer. Therefore, it can be used to change the layer to 'Cut' only after applying '**Fill**.'

- **Print:** This is used to access color and pattern options when using '**Print and Cut**."

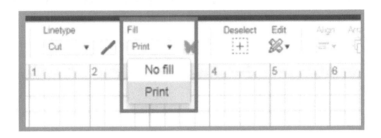

Fill Swatch:

This is used when you intend to choose additional 'Fill' attributes for the image layer, including color and patterns for 'Print Then Cut' images.

Fill attributes: Suppose you Select Print in fill; you will need to select a color or pattern fill for the image.

- **Original Artwork:** This option is used to restore a 'Print' layer to its original state, thereby removing any editing work you do.

- **Color:** This is used to select the 'Print then Cut' color from the basic color palette, custom color picker, current material colors, or inputting the hex color code.

- **Pattern:** You can use this tool to add pattern fill to text layers or images. You have the option to narrow down your search for patterns by filtering the color. Once you have found the desired pattern, you can use the 'Edit Pattern' tools to adjust its scale and orientation within the image.

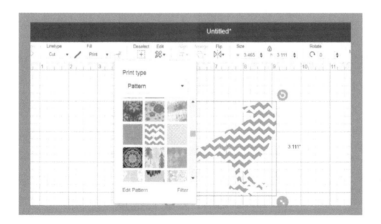

Select All/Deselect:

To select or deselect all items on the canvas at once, use this option.

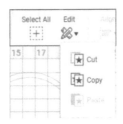

Edit:

This is used to find normal editing tools, including cut, copy and paste. Use the Cut option to remove an image from the clipboard to paste later; The Copy option is used to copy an image; The Paste option is used to paste a copied or cut image from the clipboard onto the canvas.

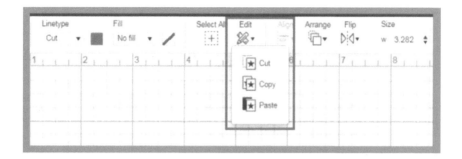

Align:

This is used to position two or more images/objects using a defined margin. You can line up the images to the left, right, top or bottom, and center (horizontally or vertically). Under this tool are some options as described below.

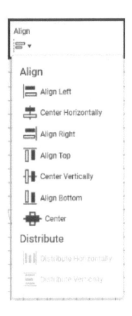

- **Align Left:** With this option, you can position two or more images/objects using the left margin. The leftmost edge of the object on the canvas feels its effect.

- **Align Right:** With this option, you can position two or more objects using the right margin. The right-most edge of the right-most object of the selected feels the effect of this option when you click it.

- **Align Top:** This option positions images/objects using the top margin. The topmost edge of selected objects/images will feel its effect.

- **Align Bottom:** With this option, you can position two or more images/objects using the bottom margin, and the bottom-most edge of the bottom-most selected objects will feel its effect.

- **Center:** This option is used to line up all the central points of the selected objects. It is also used to stack images on top of each other.

- **Center Horizontally:** This defines the horizontal center point of two or more objects/images, and its effect is felt by the exact horizontal center of selected images/objects (the central point).

- **Center Vertically:** This option is used to position two or more images/objects using the vertical center margin. The central point will be the exact vertical center of the selected objects/images, where its effect will be felt when you click this option.

- **Distribute Horizontally:** You can position the selected images to be evenly distributed between the left and right edges of the objects that you selected.

- **Distribute Vertically:** This option is used to position the selected objects to be evenly distributed between the topmost and bottom-most edges of the objects that you selected.

Arrange:

You use this feature to adjust the arrangement of objects on the Canvas by using the options to Move to Back, Move Backward, Move to Front, and Move Forward. Any changes you make will be shown in the Layers Panel.

- **Send to Back:** Like the name, it is used to send the selected object to the back of the stack according to the order of stacking. Therefore, the object will move to the bottom of the Layers Panel.

- **Move Backward:** This option moves the selected object one layer to the back according to the stacking order.

- **Move Forward:** With this option, you can move the selected object one step (layer) forward according to the stacking order. Therefore, the object moves one layer forward in the 'Layers Panel.'

- **Send to Front:** This moves the selected object to the front according to the stacking order. This will make the object appear at the top of the Layers Panel.

Flip:

This feature is used to flip an object horizontally or vertically.

- Flip Horizontal: To flip an object horizontally, place the center of the object as the pivot point.

- Flip Vertical: Flip an object vertically at the center of the object.

Size:

If you need to change the size of an object, you have two options. You can enter a specific value for its width or height or use the stepper to make adjustments in 0.1 increments.

Rotate:

Rotating your image on your canvas is pretty simply with the rotate tool located to the top right of the editing square, which is around the image when it's selected. To adjust the angle of your object, you can either enter an exact degree or use the stepper to adjust it by one degree at a time.

On the Edit Bar is a section labeled "**Rotate**" with small up and down arrows that can be used to adjust your image's orientation. By clicking these arrows, you can turn your image incrementally. Clicking **up** will rotate it to the **right** while clicking **down** will rotate it to the **left**.

Additionally, it is possible to adjust the angle of rotation precisely, ensuring that it is perfectly straight or at an exact angle. To set the angle of your image or font, enter the desired degree value into the number box.

NOTE: If "Rotate" and "Position" are missing, they sometimes like to hide under the "More" button.

More:

If your screen resolution is too narrow, some tools on the Edit bar may not be visible. In such cases, a "More" drop-down menu will appear.

Position:

To adjust the position of your object, you can either enter an exact distance from the top left corner of the Canvas or use the stepper to adjust the distance by increments of 0.1.

Placing Text or Images on Design Screen:

To change the linetype, go to the 'Edit' bar and click on the 'Linetype' drop-down. The current linetype will be highlighted.

If you want to change the linetype of multiple layers, select the layers and choose the desired linetype from the drop-down. Your selection will be reflected in the canvas image once you have made the change.

To utilize the 'Print then Cut' option, click on the 'Fill' drop-down and choose 'Print.' Select 'Color' or 'Pattern' from the 'Fill' swatch drop-down if you want to include a color or pattern in the layer.

When using the 'Write' or 'Score' linetype in a project with multiple layers, it is necessary to attach the image to another layer. To do this, select both layers in the 'Layers' panel and click the 'Attach' button.

How to Perform Linetype from Android/iOS

- To begin, add your text or images to the design screen.

- Then, navigate to the Layers panel by tapping on the 'Layers' button at the bottom of the screen.

- Once you are in the Layers panel, click the arrow next to the layer to access the 'Layer Attributes' panel.

- You will see that the current linetype is high-lighted. Choose the linetype you want by tapping on it.

- Finally, if you have finished selecting your line-type, tap on the 'Layers' button again to close the panel.

Working with Fonts in Design Space:

Cricut Design Space offers a unique feature of personalizing projects with distinct fonts and text. This feature allows you to express your creativity freely, tapping into your innate creative ability. The satisfaction and sense of accomplishment of delivering projects to your taste are unparalleled.

Cricut Design Space has an incredible feature that allows you to change the font even after ungrouping or isolating letters. You can use either the Cricut fonts or those installed on your computer or device.

Let's explore how to add text, select fonts, and install/uninstall them on Windows/Mac, one step at a time.

Adding Text to Cricut Design Space:

To access the 'Text' tool, go to the left-hand side of the canvas. If you're using the iOS or Android app, you'll find it at the bottom-left of the screen.

Once you've selected the text tool, iOS/Android users will see the font list appear, while Windows/Mac users will see the text bar and text box appear.

Please choose the font size and type that you would like to use before inputting your text. If you want to start a new line within the same textbox, press the "Return" key after typing out the previous line.

How to Edit Text in Cricut Design Space:

You can adjust the text's size, placement, and even rotation. Here's an easy guide to editing text on the canvas.

Editing text is a straightforward process—Double-click on the text to reveal the available options. From there, you can choose the action you want to perform, including changing the font style.

Using the Edit bar, you can adjust the font type, font size, letter spacing, and line spacing. The Edit bar is found at the top of the canvas for Windows/Mac users and at the bottom of the canvas for iOS/Android users.

How to Select Fonts:

If you are familiar with the 'Image Edit Tool,' then you will easily navigate the 'Text Edit Tool' in Cricut Design Space.

The reason for their similarity is that both tools operate similarly by rotating, sizing, and positioning text. This similarity is helpful as it simplifies the task of editing text and finding the appropriate font. As a result, it becomes easier to personalize projects.

Are you familiar with the bounding box? If not, let me explain. The bounding box is the rectangular outline that surrounds your selected text. It serves as a boundary for the text box and has round handles on each corner. These handles allow for easy text editing, such as rotating, resizing, deleting, and locking or unlocking the aspect ratio.

In Cricut Design Space, the Edit bar allows you to customize the features of specific images or text. These features include linetype, size, rotation, fill, positioning, and mirroring. You can also adjust line spacing, font styles, and letter spacing when working with text layers. If you're wondering how to edit the font, I can guide you through the process.

To edit a text object on the canvas, select it. You can also insert text from the design panel or choose a text layer from the 'Layers Panel.' Once selected, the 'Text Edit Bar' will appear below the 'Standard Edit Bar.' Keep in mind that the 'Standard Edit Bar' will disappear when you're not interacting with the text.

Font Filter:

You can select your preferred font type from the options available in the 'Font Type' menu, categorized by different categories. There are various font filters available, which are explained further below.

- **All Fonts:** This displays all the available fonts for you.

- **System Fonts:** This display the fonts found on your computer.

- **Cricut Fonts:** This displays fonts from the Cricut library.

- **Single-Layer Fonts:** These display fonts containing just one layer.

- **Writing Style Fonts:** This display specifically designed fonts that are written with a pen.

Style:

You can choose from various font styles, such as italic, bold, regular, bold italic, and writing style. Please keep in mind that the available style options may vary depending on whether you are using a Cricut font or a System Font.

Font Size:

This option allows you to alter the size of the font using the point size. You can type the point size value or use steppers to change the value incrementally.

Letter Space:

This allows you to alter the space between letters. Like the font size, you can type in the value or use the steppers.

Line Space:

This enables you to change the spacing between rows of text. Again, you can type in the value or use the steppers, as discussed previously.

Alignment:

This allows you to position the entire block of text to the left, right, or center, or even full justification.

Curve:

This enables you to bend the text into a circular shape. This is a good option for a crafter who designed write-ups for curved materials, such as tumblers, bowls, and buckets.

CHAPTER FOURTEEN

The Layer Panel is a crucial component of the design interface that allows you to manage and organize your projects' elements easily. In this chapter, you will learn more about the layer panel in Cricut Design Space.

When you create or import a design, each individual element is represented as a separate layer in the Layer Panel. This panel provides a comprehensive view of all the layers present in your design, enabling you to control their arrangement, visibility, and other properties.

At the right of the Canvas, reaching from top to bottom is the Layers Panel. Using the Layer Panel effectively allows you to manage complex designs efficiently, maintain an organized workflow, and achieve the precise results you envision. Here's what to expect in the Layer Panel:

You'll see four commands at the top of the Layers Panel. These commands are Group, Ungroup, Duplicate, and Delete. At the bottom, you'll see five more options. They are Slice, Weld, Flatten, Attach, and Contour.

Group/Ungroup:

Grouping items allows you to combine multiple elements into a single unit, making it easier to manipulate and move them as a cohesive whole. To group an item, click your mouse cursor to create a selection box around the elements you want to group.

Alternatively, you can hold the Shift key while clicking on individual elements to select multiple items. Once the desired elements are selected, tap the **Group icon** in the layer panel.

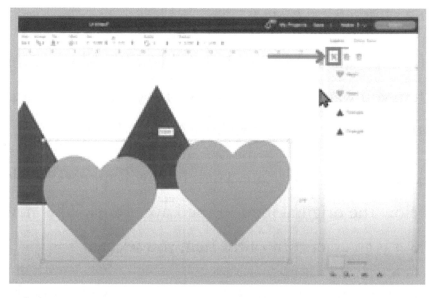

After grouping, you'll notice that the selected elements are now enclosed within a bounding box with handles. This indicates that they have been successfully grouped into a single layer. Ungroup merely separates that which has been grouped so it can be moved separately once more.

Duplicate:

Duplicating an item is a simple process that allows you to create multiple copies of the same design element. This feature is handy for repeating an element or creating symmetrical designs.

To duplicate an item, you must identify and select the item you want to replicate in the Layer Panel. The next step is to click on the duplicate icon in the layer panel.

After selecting duplicate, a new layer will appear directly below the original item in the Layer Panel. This new layer is an exact copy of the item you selected.

You can continue duplicating the item by clicking the duplicate icon at the layer panel. Each time you duplicate the element, a new layer will be added to the Layer Panel, representing an additional copy of the design element on your canvas.

You can rename the duplicated item by double-clicking on the item in the layer panel to display rename box. Enter the new name of the item, and it will be saved.

Once you have duplicated the item, you can rearrange the items in the layer panel by clicking and dragging the item layer from its current position to where you want them to be.

NOTE: To duplicate several at once, draw a box around the group you wish to duplicate. Press duplicate, and drag your duplicated group of items to another place on the Canvas.

Your items will move as a group, just as though they've been grouped together. When you click outside of the "group" area, they'll ungroup and become separate items.

Delete:

The same thing applies to "Delete" as with "Duplicate." You can delete one item at a time or a group of items at a time. If you want to delete several things simultaneously, drag a box around them and click "**Delete**."

Slice:

The slice feature allows you to divide or cut out overlapping shapes or images to create new, custom designs. When you use the Slice option, it separates the overlapping areas of selected layers and creates individual new shapes from those intersections.

This feature is handy for creating intricate designs, adding cutouts, or making unique layered patterns. It is important to note that the slice option is available under certain conditions:

- **Overlapping Layers:** To use the Slice feature, you need to have two or more layers overlapping on the canvas. For example, if you have two shapes or images placed on top of each other, the Slice option will be enabled.

- **Only Two Layers:** The Slice feature can only be used with two similar layers at a time. If you have more than two layers selected for slicing, the option will be grayed out.

To slice an item, click on the layers you want to slice to select them. You can select multiple layers by holding down the Shift key while clicking.

With the layers selected, click the "**Slice**" button at the bottom of the Layers Panel. This action will divide the selected layers into separate pieces in overlapping areas.

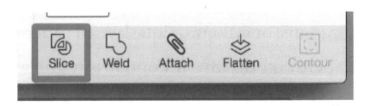

After slicing, you will see the original layers and the newly created sliced parts. Delete the unwanted overlapping parts by clicking on them and tap "**Delete**."

Combine:

The Combine feature allows you to merge multiple shapes or images into a single unified layer. When you use the Combine option, the selected layers are merged together. The options in the Combine Menu are as follows:

Weld: Welding is one of the options available in the Combine menu. Welding combines multiple overlapping shapes into a single shape, creating a new and fixed item. You can no longer alter each items individually.

To weld two or more items together, follow the process below;

- You need to make sure that both items overlap each other.

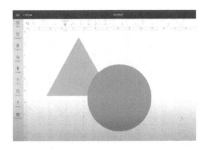

- Then select both items and click on the "**Combine**" icon at the bottom of the layer panel.

- In the context menu, select the "**Weld**" option.

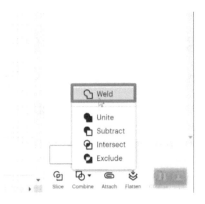

The two items will be welded together to form a single object/shape and one layer. It is important to note that when you have welded two objects and saved the project, you can not undo the action of welding again.

Unite: Unite is another option available in the Combine menu that you can use to connect two items together. The unite option merges multiple overlapping shapes into a single shape, creating a seamless and continuous design.

Unite and weld have similar functions; the major difference is that in unite, each object can be enlarged or reduced without affecting the other conjoined items. Also, the unite function keeps the individual item as a separate layer grouped together as unite rather than a fixed layer. To unite two or more items together, follow the process below;

- You need to make sure that both items overlap each other.

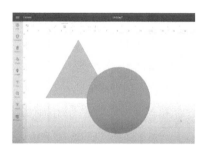

- Then select both items and click on the "**Combine**" icon at the bottom of the layer panel.

- In the context menu, select the "**Unite**" option.

On the left side of the panel, you'll noticed that the items are grouped individually

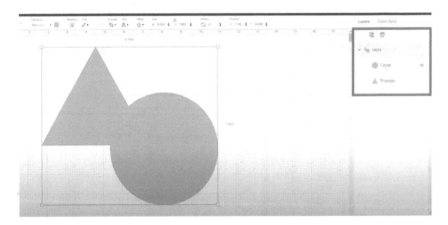

You can undo unite the items by simply selecting the items and proceed to select the **combine** option at the bottom of the layer panel. Here, you will see the option

to **Undo Unite**.

You can also weld the items that you have unite by selecting the **combine** option at the bottom of the layer panel, and tap "**Merge Layer**."

Subtract: This feature cuts out the overlapping front item from the back item. The subtract feature works similarly to the slice, but the difference is that the cutout item is not available in subtract. Here is how to use the subtract feature;

- Create two items that are overlapping each other. Ensure that the shape you want to subtract is on top of the shape you want to cut from.

- Click on the shape you want to subtract to select it. It will be highlighted with a bounding box.

- Proceed to the Layers Panel on the right side of the screen, and click on the "**Combine**" button located at the bottom.

- In the context menu, select "**Subtract**."

- After clicking on the "**Subtract**" button, the overlapping area of the selected shape will be subtracted from the shape below it; thereby creating a new shape with the cutout design.

Intersect: Intersect is another combined tool used to exclude items that are not interloping. You will only get the items that intersect one another. When you use the Intersect feature, it creates a new shape that includes only the overlapping areas of the selected layers. This is a powerful tool for creating custom shapes and intricate designs. Here's how to use the Intersect feature in the Layer Panel:

- Create a new design or shapes you want to work with on the canvas. Arrange the layers on the canvas so that they overlap as desired. The overlapping areas will be used to create the new shape.

- Click on the layers you want to intersect to select them. You can select multiple layers by holding down the Shift key while clicking. Proceed to the layer panel and select the "Combine" button at the bottom of the panel.

- In the context menu, click on the "**Intersect**" button, and this action will create a new shape that includes only the overlapping areas of the selected layers.

Exclude: The Exclude feature is used to remove or subtract the overlapping areas of two or more shapes or images, leaving behind the non-overlapping area. Here is how to use this feature:

- Position the shapes or images on the canvas so that they overlap in the desired way.

- Click on the layers you want to exclude to select them. You can select multiple layers by holding down the Shift key while clicking.

- Select the "**Combine**" button at the bottom of the layer panel.

- Locate and select the "**Exclude**" option, and the overlapping areas of the selected layers will be subtracted, leaving behind the non-overlapping areas to create a new shape.

Attach:

Attach is another option in the Combine menu. When you attach layers, they will stay in their original positions relative to each other during the cutting process. This option is particularly helpful when you want to maintain the layout and alignment of different elements in your design.

The attach feature is beneficial when you want to maintain the layout and alignment of different elements in your design. Here's how to use the Attach feature:

1. **Create or Import Design:** Either create a new

design or import the images or shapes you want to work with onto the canvas.

2. **Arrange Layers:** Position the layers on the canvas as desired, arranging them to achieve the layout you want.

3. **Select Layers:** Click on the layers you want to attach to select them. You can select multiple layers by holding down the Shift key while clicking.

4. **Click on Attach:** Once the desired layers are selected, click on the "Attach" button at the bottom of the Layers Panel. This action will group the selected layers together and keep them in their current positions relative to each other.

5. **Verify Attachment:** Once attached, you will notice that the layers are combined into a single unit in the Layers Panel, and they will be displayed as one element on the canvas.

6. **Cut or Make It:** Now that the layers are attached, you can proceed to the cutting or crafting process. Click on the "**Make It**" button to set up your material and mat settings, and then follow the on-screen instructions to complete your project.

Remember that attaching layers in Cricut Design Space affects how they will be cut on the mat, so double-check the layout before proceeding with the cutting process.

The Attach feature simplifies your crafting process and ensures that your Cricut Maker 3 creates your design exactly as you envision it.

Flatten:

The Flatten feature allows you to combine multiple layers, including images and text, into a single printable image for the Print then Cut function. This is especially useful when you want to create custom stickers, labels, or intricate designs with a patterned or printed background. Here's how to use the Flatten feature in the Layer Panel:

1. **Create or Import Design:** In the Design Space canvas, create a new design or import the images and text you want to work with onto the canvas.

2. **Arrange Layers:** Position the layers on the canvas to achieve the desired layout. Ensure that the layers you want to flatten are overlapping or placed on top of each other as needed.

3. **Select Layers:** Click on the layers you want to flatten to select them. You can select multiple layers by holding down the Shift key while clicking.

4. **Flatten:** With the layers selected, click on the "**Flatten**" button located at the bottom of the Layers Panel. This action will combine the selected layers into a single, printable image.

5. **Check the Preview:** After clicking Flatten, a preview of the flattened image will appear on the canvas. Review the preview to ensure it looks as intended.

6. **Print then Cut:** Once you're satisfied with the flattened image, proceed to the Print then Cut function. Click on the "**Make It**" button and follow the on-screen instructions to print your design on a compatible printer and then have your Cricut Maker 3 cut around the printed images.

If you are using the Print then Cut feature in Cricut Design Space, the Flatten option allows you to combine images and text with a pattern or print to create a single, printable layer. This is useful for creating custom stickers or labels with intricate designs.

Contour:

The Contour feature allows you to hide or remove specific parts of an image or shape, giving you greater control over your design. With the Contour feature, you can easily customize and edit your images, creating intricate and personalized designs for your Cricut Maker 3 projects. Here is how to use the Contour feature:

1. **Create or Import Design:** Launch the design space and select create a new design or import the image or shape you want to work with onto the canvas.

2. **Access the Contour Feature:** Once you have your design on the canvas, select the image or shape you want to modify by clicking on it. The Layers Panel will display the image's selected layer(s).

3. **Click on Contour:** In the Layers Panel, click

on the "**Contour**" button. This will open the Contour window, showing you all the individual components of the selected image or shape.

4. **Hide or Show Parts:** In the Contour window, you will see a list of the parts or layers that make up the selected image. A thumbnail image represents each part. Click on the parts you want to hide or remove from your design. The parts you click on will be grayed out, indicating that they will be hidden.

5. **Hide All Contours:** If you want to hide all the individual components of the selected image at once, you can click on the "**Hide All Contours**" button. This will remove all the components from the design, leaving you with a basic shape.

6. **Exit:** Once you have customized the design using the Contour feature, click on the "**X**" in the

top right corner of the Contour window to exit and return to the main canvas.

7. **Customize and Design:** With the desired parts hidden or removed, you can now further customize and design your project as you see fit. You can resize, rotate, and position the modified image, add text, or combine it with other shapes and images.

Color Sync Panel:

The Color Sync panel in Cricut Design Space is a helpful feature that allows you to organize and arrange different colors within your design easily. This panel is found in the Layers Panel. It is especially useful when working on projects that involve multiple layers or when you want to control the cutting order of different colors. How to Use the Color Sync Panel:

1. **Create or Import Design:** Launch the design

space and start by creating a new design or importing the image or shape you want to work with onto the canvas.

2. **Layer Colors:** As you add shapes or images to your canvas, each element will be displayed as a separate layer in the Layers Panel. By default, Cricut Design Space assigns random colors to each layer.

3. **Access Color Sync:** To access the Color Sync feature, click the "**Color Sync**" button at the bottom of the Layers Panel. This will open the Color Sync panel.

4. **Organize Colors:** In the Color Sync panel, you will see all the layers of your design displayed as color swatches. You can click and drag these swatches to rearrange the layers and organize them according to your preferred color sequence.

5. **Change Colors:** If you want to change the color of a particular layer, you can click on the color swatch and choose a new color from the color palette that appears. This feature is especially useful when coordinating colors or creating specific color themes in your project.

6. **Cut Order:** The Color Sync panel also affects the cut order of your layers. The layers are cut in the order they appear in the Color Sync panel from top to bottom. This means the top layer will be cut first, followed by the layers below.

7. **Save Changes:** Once you have organized the colors and layers to your satisfaction, click on the "Done" button in the Color Sync panel to save your changes and return to the main canvas.

How to Change Canvas Color:

The Color Sync panel in Cricut Design Space is a helpful feature that allows you to organize and arrange different colors within your design easily.

This panel is found in the Layers Panel. It is especially useful when working on projects that involve multiple layers or when you want to control the cutting order of different colors. How to Use the Color Sync Panel:

1. **Open Cricut Design Space:** Launch Cricut Design Space on your computer or mobile device and log in to your account.

2. **Create Design:** Start by creating a new design or importing the image or shape you want to work with onto the canvas.

3. **Layer Colors:** As you add shapes or images to your canvas, each element will be displayed as a separate layer in the Layers Panel. By default,

Cricut Design Space assigns random colors to each layer.

4. **Access Color Sync:** To access the Color Sync feature, click the "**Color Sync**" button at the bottom of the Layers Panel. This will open the Color Sync panel.

5. **Organize Colors:** In the Color Sync panel, you will see all the layers of your design displayed as color swatches. You can click and drag these swatches to rearrange the layers and organize them according to your preferred color sequence.

6. **Change Colors:** If you want to change the color of a particular layer, you can click on the color swatch and choose a new color from the color palette that appears. This feature is especially useful when coordinating colors or creating specific color themes in your project.

7. **Cut Order:** The Color Sync panel also affects the cut order of your layers. The layers are cut in the order they appear in the Color Sync panel from top to bottom. This means the top layer will be cut first, followed by the layers below.

CHAPTER FIFTEEN

Design Space Tips

Design Space in Cricut is like a spice that adds flavor to your design in the Cricut, and it's one of the most important tools for getting the most out of your Cricut machine. Here are a few tips that will be useful;

How to use Color Sync Panel

In Cricut Design Space, the Color Sync panel allows you to match the colors of your project to a specific color palette or brand. To use the Color Sync panel:

- Open the project you want to work on in Cricut Design Space.

- Select the "*Canvas*" tab on the right side.

- Click on the "***Color Sync***" panel, which is located in the "Layers" section of the right sidebar.

- In the Color Sync panel, you will see a list of the colors used in your project, as well as a list of color palettes and brands that you can choose from.

- Select the palette or brand from the list to match the colors in your project to a specific color palette or brand.

- Cricut Design Space will automatically update the colors in your project to match the selected palette or brand.

- If you want to customize the colors in your project, you can click on any of the colors in the Color Sync panel

- When you're finished, click "***Apply***" to save your changes.

How to Use Patterns in Cricut Design Space

Pattern is a feature used to fill any text or image layers in Cricut Design Space. It is important to know that there are numerous patterns in the Cricut Design Space pattern library. If you do not like any of the patterns, you can customize or upload your own pattern. Here is how to use patterns;

- Open the project you want to work on in Cricut Design Space.

- Select the *"Canvas"* tab on the right side of the screen.

- Click on the *"Layers"* panel in the right sidebar.

- In the Layers panel, select the layer that you want to apply a pattern to.

- Click on the *"Fill"* dropdown menu in the Layers panel, and select "*Pattern*."

- A list of available patterns will appear. Scroll through the list and select the pattern you want to use.

- The pattern will be applied to the selected layer.

- If you want to customize the pattern, click on the "*Customize*" button next to the pattern name. This will open the Pattern Options panel, where you can adjust the size, alignment, and orientation of the pattern.

- When you're finished, click "*Apply*" to save your changes.

How to Mirror Designs

During the heat transfer process, your iron-on design will be protected by the shiny, clear, heat-resistant liner that is attached to most iron-on materials. Your machine can only cut your pattern if the liner is facing down. Consequently, before you begin cutting, you'll want to make a mirror image of your design in Design Space. Here is how to go about the process;

- Once you have finished customizing your design and are ready to cut, click on the *"Make It"* button to proceed to the project preview.

- If you have any design elements intended for heat transfer, make sure to toggle the *"Mirror"* switch on for each load type. Then, click *"Continue"* to complete your cut.

- If you forget to mirror your design and select a heat-transfer material setting, Design Space will remind you to do so. To fix this, click "*Edit*" and toggle the "*Mirror*" switch on, then select "*Done*." Repeat this process for each load type as needed.

- Once you have finished these steps, you are ready to cut your design.

Working with Text in Design Space

For new text to be added to Canvas, click the Text icon. A text box with the word "Text" highlighted. The text is in edit mode when it appears like this. To update your text, begin to type.

How to Modify Text:

The Edit mode ends if you click anywhere other than the text field, but making changes is simple;

- Double-click on your text, and choose Edit Text

from the menu to add new words or make edits.

- Another option is to use the Edit menu's feature, or by right-clicking within the text box, you may cut, copy, and paste while the letter(s) are chosen.

How to Rotate Text

You can rotate the text box on a canvas by using any corner handle of a bounding box or by entering a number in the Rotate input field in the Edit toolbar.

Allow the pointer to hover slightly beyond the corner handle of the bounding box while rotating until a curving arrow emerges. Rotate the text by clicking and dragging.

Sizing a Text

Text may be resized by dragging any corner handle on the bounding box or by entering values in the Size input boxes on the Edit toolbar. In the Edit toolbar, click the

Lock symbol to unlock proportions so you may separately alter the width and height.

Resizing the text box

You don't have to modify the font size you've chosen to change the size of the box your text is in. Click and move the bounding box's main rectangular handles. By default, the text is aligned horizontally and vertically, but you can change the text position by using the Alignment, Letter Space, and Line Space tools.

Text Wrapping

By default, just one line of text is put to the canvas. No line breaks are necessary; depending on the size of your text box, you may have your text wrap or flow to a new line.

Click and drag a center rectangular handle on the text box to move a word to a new line or bring a word back from the previous line. Your text box enters wrap mode as a result. Select Wrap Off from the Alignment menu to get out of the Wrap mode.

How to Curve Text

You may shape-shift your text into a circle with the Curve tool. To discover how to curve text in Design Space, go to this help page.

How to Delete Text

Use the delete keys on the keyboard to remove text.

Design Space Tricks

Here are a few tips and tricks for using Cricut Design Space:

- Use the "**Duplicate**" option to create multiple copies of an object quickly. This is especially useful for creating repeating patterns or for making small adjustments to multiple copies of the same object.

- Use the "**Group**" and "**Ungroup**" options to manipulate multiple objects as a single unit.

This is useful for moving and resizing multiple objects at once.

- Use the "**Align**" and "**Distribute**" options to quickly and easily align multiple objects. These options allow you to align objects by their edges and centers or evenly distribute them across a page.

- Use the "**Weld**" option to merge two or more shapes into a single object. This is useful for creating more complex shapes or for combining text and images.

- Use the "**Contour**" option to cut out a shape or design from a larger object. This is useful for creating intricate cuts or for creating a "negative" version of a shape.

- Use the "**Flip**" option to quickly and easily reverse an object horizontally or vertically. This is useful for creating mirrored images or adjusting an object's orientation.

- Use the **"Fill"** and **"Outline"** options to add color to your designs. The Fill option allows you to add color to the inside of an object, while the Outline option allows you to add color to the outline of an object.

- Use the **"Layers"** panel to organize your designs and keep track of which objects are on top or behind others. This is especially useful for creating multi-layered designs or for adjusting the visibility of different objects.

CHAPTER SIXTEEN

Cricut Access Subscription Plan

There needs to be more clarity out there concerning Cricut Access. Many people will claim why it is important, and you need it, and some people will say that you don't. In this chapter, you will learn about Cricut Access and how to get started with it.

I was so puzzled about this topic that I did a lot of homework to understand it and its functions better. There was no single research on this subject that could address any of my concerns. Now, I will explain what Cricut Access is before diving in:

What is Cricut Access?

It is a premium subscription that allows you immediate access to an awesome and vast library full of over 90,000 pictures, more than a hundred fonts, and many projects ready to be sliced. Based on your package, you will get some perks, such as discounts on approved fonts, images, and actual items.

How Is Cricut Access Different from The Cricut Design Space?

The question confuses a lot of people. Many people, including myself, needed clarification on Cricut Access with the Design Space in the early days.

The differentiation between the Design Space and the Cricut Access is that the Design Space is a Free program where you import, edit, and eventually submit your designs to be cut to your machine.

The Access is a premium subscription full of designs that you can use inside the Cricut Design Space that are graphics, fonts, and ready to cut.

If you do not have a premium membership for Cricut Access, you can still use all the graphics provided in Cricut Design Space. However, when submitting your idea for a cutting, you may need to account for the digital data involved. Whether something costs money or not, it is easy to understand.

If you wish to avoid paying or having access to Cricut, it is best to avoid those projects. You can upload your own sketches, use your own fonts, and even create simple designs using shapes such as squares, triangles, hearts, etc., all within Cricut Design Space and at no cost.

Do You Need Cricut Access?

From my perspective, having Cricut Access is beneficial if you're unfamiliar with creating or constructing your designs and prefer to avoid searching for free options.

It allows for more frequent use of your device. I find joy in designing and building my own creations, which is why I purchased a Cricut. Cutting designs is made easier with it. The pleasure for me lies in the design process.

Pros and Cons Of The Cricut Access

If you still cannot decide on having or not having Cricut Access. Perhaps these advantages and disadvantages are going to help you eventually decide:

Pros:

- It allows you to use the device more often.

- Learning and performing beautiful tasks simultaneously is so much better for you.

- You get additional discounts on machines, materials, and accessories from the Cricut website.

- You don't require some previous knowledge to create something unique.

- Find almost everything you like for any reason, any time of the year.

Cons:

- Cricut access is a chronic cost. After you quit paying, you would only have unrestricted access to some of the previews used with fonts or icons.

- Only inside the Design Space can you use them. Forget to use other applications, including Inkscape or Adobe Illustrator, to combine specific fonts and pictures.

Are there any other alternatives for Access?

You require Cricut Design Space if you want to cut your designs. However, you can have your files cut and then upload those files.

Plans of Cricut Access Explained

Cricut Access is an optional subscription plan that provides access to a library of images, fonts, and projects for use with Cricut Design Space. There are two plans available:

- **Standard:** This plan costs $7.99 per month or $79.99 per year. It includes access to over 250,000 images, 700 fonts, and thousands of projects.

- **Premium:** This plan costs $9.99 per month or $99.99 per year. It includes everything in the

Standard plan, plus access to exclusive features and discounts on Cricut products.

CHAPTER SEVENTEEN

Project Ideas for Beginners

Several projects can be done with your Cricut explore 3. In this chapter, you will learn about several Cricut projects you can complete in 2023. Here are some Cricut project ideas to get you started:

Christmas Project Ideas:

- Christmass gift tags

- Festive garlands

- Christmas T-shirts

- Christmass Calendars

- Christmas cards and boxes

- Christmas tree skirt

- Customized Christmas stockings

- Festive holiday table settings, including place cards and napkin rings

- Customized holiday signs and banners to hang around your home

Thanksgiving Project Ideas:

- Customized place cards

- Decorated table runners

- Thanksgiving-themed shirts

- Personalized cutting board

- Gratitude journal

- Personalized welcome mat

- Decorated tablecloths

- Festive paper napkin rings

- Decorated tea towels

Mother's Day Project Ideas:

- Personalized tote bags

- Customized picture frames

- Decorated mugs

- Handmade cards

- Mother's Day-themed shirts

- Embroidered hand towels

- DIY floral arrangements

- Monogrammed coasters

- Decorated picture frames

- Customized stationery

Father's Day Project Idea's:

- Customized hats

- Customized beer glasses

- Monogrammed leather keychains

- Father's Day-themed shirts

- Decorated coffee mugs

- Personalized photo frames

- Monogrammed bathrobes

- Decorated beer bottle openers

Wedding Project Idea's:

- Personalized wedding invitations

- Customized table numbers

- Wedding-themed shirts for the bride/groom party

- Customized cake topper

- Customized guest book

- Customized signs and banners

- Personalized hangers for the bridal party

- Decorated wedding shoe decals

- Customized wedding cake server set

- Customized wedding seating chart

Birthday Gift Ideas:

- Personalized photo albums

- Customized birthday cards

- DIY birthday banners

- Personalized tote bags

- Customized coffee mugs

- Handmade birthday cake toppers

- Personalized birthday shirts

- DIY birthday crowns

- DIY cake stands

- Customized birthday wrapping paper.

CHAPTER EIGHTEEN

Maintaining Cricut Explore 3

The Cricut Explore 3 is a powerful cutting machine that can help you create beautiful and intricate designs for various crafting projects. However, to ensure that it functions optimally and lasts for a long time, it's essential to take good care of it.

Proper maintenance of your Cricut Explore 3 can help prevent damage, ensure clean and precise cuts, and increase its lifespan. In this chapter, we will explore the different ways to maintain your Cricut Explore 3, including cleaning the machine regularly, using high-quality materials, using the correct blade, and having it serviced regularly.

By following these advice, you can keep your Cricut Explore 3 in excellent condition and create stunning designs for years to come. Here are some ways to maintain your Cricut Explore 3:

Clean Cricut Explore Regularly:

Cleaning your Cricut Explore 3 regularly is essential to maintain its functionality and longevity. The exterior of the machine and the cutting mat should be wiped down with a clean, dry cloth after every use to remove dust and debris.

You can also use a mild cleaning solution to wipe down the machine's exterior if necessary, but make sure that the solution is safe for use on the machine's materials.

It's also important to clean the rollers on the machine regularly to prevent dust and debris buildup, which can cause the material to slip during cutting. To clean the rollers, use a soft cloth or sponge dipped in warm, soapy water and wipe down each roller individually.

When cleaning the cutting mat, avoid using harsh cleaning solutions or abrasive materials that can damage the mat's surface. Instead, use a soft-bristled brush to remove any debris from the mat's surface, or gently wipe it down with a damp cloth.

Regular cleaning of your Cricut Explore 3 not only helps to keep it in good working order but also helps to prevent damage to the machine and the materials you are cutting. By taking the time to clean your machine regularly, you can ensure that it remains a reliable tool for your crafting needs.

Use Dust Cover:

Using a dust cover for your Cricut Explore 3 is an essential part of maintaining the machine. A dust cover is a protective cover that helps prevent dust, dirt, and other debris from settling on the machine and its components.

These covers are usually made of durable, water-resistant materials and are designed to fit the Cricut Explore 3 perfectly. Dust can be a significant issue for cutting machines like the Cricut Explore 3.

Dust particles can accumulate on the machine's rollers and blades, affecting its performance and causing damage. A dust cover protects the machine from these particles, keeping it clean and functioning smoothly.

Furthermore, a dust cover can protect the machine from scratches and other physical damage. When the machine is not in use, it may be tempting to stack items on top of it, but a dust cover will discourage this behavior and keep the machine free from unnecessary wear and tear.

Store the Machine Properly:

Proper storage of your Cricut Explore 3 is essential to protect it from dust, moisture, and other environmental factors that can cause damage or malfunction.

When storing your machine, it's crucial to choose a clean, dry, and secure location that is away from direct sunlight or heat sources. Additionally, consider investing in a dust cover to further protect your machine from debris and environmental factors.

When storing the Cricut Explore 3, it's also important to ensure that it is positioned in a level and upright position. Avoid stacking anything heavy on top of the machine or storing it in a location where it can be knocked over.

Make sure the storage area is also free of any potential hazards that can cause damage to the machine. It's recommended that you store the Cricut Explore 3 in its original box or a storage container that fits its dimensions to provide additional protection.

Make sure that any accessories, such as blades and mats, are stored alongside the machine in a clean and dry location. By taking the time to store your Cricut Explore 3 properly, you can help ensure that it remains in excellent condition and is ready to use when you need it.

Proper storage can also prevent unnecessary wear and tear on the machine, which can prolong its lifespan and save you money in the long run.

Use High-quality Materials:

The Cricut Explore Air 3 is a cutting machine that is capable of cutting a wide range of materials such as vinyl, cardstock, paper, and fabric. These materials come in various grades and thicknesses, and using low-quality materials can result in poor-quality cuts, difficulty in weeding, and poor adhesion.

Using high-quality materials ensures that the Cricut Explore Air 3 cuts precisely and cleanly, resulting in a polished and professional-looking finished product. High-quality materials are more durable and resistant to wear and tear, which is particularly important when creating items that are intended for long-term use.

Maintenance Tips:

Here are some maintenance tips to adhere to in order to keep your Cricut Explorer safe;

- **Don't overload the mat:** Don't overload the mat with too much material as this can damage the machine.

- **Use the correct blade:** Use the correct blade for the material you are cutting to ensure clean cuts.

- **Don't force the material:** Don't force the material through the machine as this can damage the machine.

- **Use a proper cutting technique:** Use a proper cutting technique to prevent the material from tearing or becoming misaligned.

- **Keep the rollers clean:** Clean the rollers regularly with a soft cloth to prevent dust and debris from building up.

- **Don't use a dull blade:** Replace the blade regularly to prevent damage to the machine.

- **Keep the machine dry:** Avoid exposing the machine to moisture as this can cause damage.

- **Don't use the machine for anything other than cutting:** Don't use the machine for anything other than cutting as this can damage the machine.

About the author

Shelli Lynne has been using Cricut for over five years to make unique things for her shop, and she specializes in personalized gifts and home decor. Aside from meeting family needs, she spends most of her time using the Cricut machine to craft amazing projects for her customers.

Shelli is married and a mother of two (2) children. She loves teaching, so she decided to share her knowledge and excitement in this book, which tells readers everything they need to know to use Cricut Design Space to make their own unique projects. No matter how long you've been using your Cricut, these pages will help you learn new things and get ideas.

Made in United States
Troutdale, OR
01/14/2025